THE CHAPTER
PRESIDENT

PREPARING SORORITY AND FRATERNITY LEADERS

FOR THE UNEXPECTED

BY

PATRICK DALEY

AUTHOR OF THE FRATERNITY LEADER: MAKE YOUR
· CHAPTER THE BEST ON CAMPUS

This book is dedicated to Matty, Jim, Bob, and Cuz.
You guys are RWSSNN!

TABLE OF CONTENTS

FOREWORD

My goal is to help you improve your fraternity or sorority. That is why I write.

I come at this from a uniquely, un-unique perspective. I am just an alumnus of my chapter. I am not a chapter adviser. I am not in student development. I do not hold a leadership position in my fraternity. I don't desire any of those positions. As a result, I don't have to answer to anyone.

I am just a guy who is trying to help.

I have helped by sharing my thoughts and experiences on www. thefraternityadvisor.com for the past few years. My hope is that the website will help people who are struggling with leadership issues in the Greek community. I have been overwhelmed by the site's popularity. As I write this in the summer of 2013, over a million people have visited the site. I cannot describe how rewarding this journey has been for me.

In actuality, though, the journey started long ago when I was an undergraduate brother in my chapter. From the outside, I appeared to be very successful. I was a two-year chapter president and North Carolina State University's IFC president. I was my chapter's brother of the year, NC State's Greek Man of the Year, and my fraternity's national man of the year. I was elected to be the lone undergraduate member on my fraternity's international executive council.

Despite the positions I held and the recognition I received, I was woefully unprepared to be the leader of my chapter. I was blindsided by a multitude of issues. My unpreparedness led to too many spur-of-the-moment decisions. Some were good; some were not good. I know that most chapter presidents share this experience.

I wrote this book as a road map to help chapter presidents navigate the potential pitfalls they may face. Each chapter of the book starts with a situation described by a reader of www.thefraternityadvisor.com. All forty have the potential to derail your chapter if not handled properly.

I sincerely appreciate your taking the time to read my book. If you find it to be of value, I would appreciate it if you left positive feedback on Amazon. This will ensure that future Greek leaders will be able to find the book and benefit from it during their terms as chapter president.

Fraternally,

Pat Daley

ACKNOWLEDGEMENTS

A large number of people have signed up for my e-mail list through www.thefraternityadvisor.com. When I was brainstorming ideas for this book, I asked them what topics should be included.

I received a ton of great feedback, and I used it as the introduction to each chapter.

I sincerely appreciate the insight of the following people and consider them key contributors to the book:

T. Joseph Russo, Dennis Nall, Reggie Paquette, David Stollman, Charles DeNault, Christine O' Brien, Jason Walker, Ian Cartmill, Douglas Allen, Thomas Fox, Cathy of CARDDS, Christopher Jarvis, Victor Em, Sam Fisher, Aysen Ulupinar, Rute Hill, Alex Janssen, Justin Kaplan, Josh Cherok, Ryan Lunka, Richard Adams, Chuck Pankenier, Miguel Alvarado, Reynaldo Morales, Lane French, Richard Campbell, Kevn Sigillito, Abby Rainer, Benjamin Struemph, Scott McCrae, Shaun Murphy, Matthew Brinton, Mohamed Saber, Sebastian Conn, Brent Ashley, AJ Agrawal, Alvin Blackshear, Jim Kerbow, Paul Lattan, Matthew Weber, Joshua Rose, Adam Cheek, Ryan Zanardi, Samuel Snyder, Bill Robinson, Danny Phan, Sean Murphy, Roger Wert, Chris Centi, Emilee Danielson, Leif Hadden, Dariyen Carter, Kyle Boers, Tj Nelson, Alex Gerchow, Kevin Moriles, Frankie Gonzales, Robert

Carlton, Tyler Micek, Jim Yemm, Caden Gillespie, Andrew Hart, Jorge Rodriguez, William Bringham, Jay Maguire, Cory Klein, Quinten Howze, John S. Elmaraghy, Ryan Rabac, Jaron Brandon, Mick Dean, Michael Gallagher, Chris Drew, Hoang Dinh, Brad Smith, Kyle Hartman, Stephen Oetting, Skip Cramond, David Fine, Aaron Bercovitch, Douglas Allen, Jim Kerbow, James Boyer, Rob Coan, Rob Ulmer, Matt Daley, Tim Rectanus, Daniel Skinner, Will Mansard, Pete Cusack, Ryan Young, Greg Barr, and Ryan "Cuz" Shevland.

MONEY MATTERS

MEMBERS WHO FAIL TO PAY DUES

A PERENNIAL ISSUE IS NONPAYMENT OF
FINES AND DUES. MY PRESIDENT AND
OFFICERS TOLD ME LATE IN THE SEMESTER
THAT THE CHAPTER WAS OWED AROUND
$20,000 BY BROTHERS—MANY OF WHOM
SIMPLY MISMANAGED THEIR OWN CASH
AND LEFT THE FRATERNITY HANGING OUT
TO DRY. I'D LOVE SOME INPUT ABOUT HOW
TO DEAL WITH THIS SITUATION, OTHER
THAN DROPPING THE HAMMER HARD ON
THE MEMBERS WHO GET BEHIND.

This is a huge issue in new chapters or chapters that aren't run professionally. Nothing would upset me off more than seeing a fraternity brother blow tons of money at the bar every weekend when I know he's thousands of dollars in debt to the chapter. Here are the eight steps you need to take to make sure your members stay current on their dues.

First, you need to make sure that chapter members feel they are getting value for the dues they are paying. Not only is that an essential goal for you as a leader, it is common sense. If your members believe they are getting a good return on their dues investment, they are more likely to pay.

Second, chapter expenditures must be transparent. By that, I mean that everyone in the chapter should know where the money is going. This means that the treasurer actually has to do his job and report to the chapter how the money is being spent every week. Doing so also tells the membership how much money the chapter needs to accomplish its goals. If these goals are important to the chapter — and they should be — then members will be more eager to pay their dues.

Third, members need to have a financial incentive to pay. If you can give a nominal discount for paying early, then it may be in your best interest to do so. This is actually the exact same thing as having a fine for late payment, but it is much more palatable to the membership.

Fourth, you need to ask for dues professionally. You do this by sending a dues statement to every member, every semester. In this statement, make it clear when dues are due and how to pay. You also need to send a receipt when you receive payment.

Fifth, make it easy to pay. I am not a huge fan of dues-collection companies because of the fees they charge. I just don't think the chapter needs to incur these fees to collect. The treasurer should always take a payment. He should never say, "Pay me later." The chapter should also be able to collect electronically via PayPal or similar services.

Sixth, collect promissory notes from members who do not pay on time. This note should include the member's payment plan, which spells out when he will make good on his debt. Be sure to do a quick Google check on promissory notes to see whether your state requires that they include specific information.

Seventh, the treasurer's weekly report must include the dues owed to the chapter. The amount owed by each offending member must be specified. Peer pressure will do wonders to get members to pay. If members are offended by being called out, then there is a very easy solution to their problem. They can pay their dues on time.

Eighth, make sure the chapter bylaws include a clear policy on what happens if a member does not pay his dues. The last thing you want is the offending member to accuse you of playing favorites because of an inconsistent policy. Fines and suspension of privileges should be included in this policy.

The final stage of this policy should be terminating membership and sending the offending person's debt to a collection agency. If you have the promissory note, you will have all the paperwork you need.

This eight-point procedure may seem harsh, but there is a huge culture difference between collecting dues as a club vs. as a professional organization.

Don't forget for a second that the members who are not paying their dues on time are mooching off the chapter. They are not meeting their obligations. If you don't hold them accountable, you are actually doing them a disservice. What happens when they enter the real world and don't pay their bills or mortgage? By forcing them to uphold the commitments they make in college, you are preparing them to be financially responsible for life.

THE DREADED TASK OF FUNDRAISING

> MY CHAPTER IS SMALL AND NOT COMPRISED OF A BUNCH OF RICH KIDS. MOST OF US HAVE JOBS, AND IT IS A STRUGGLE FOR A LOT OF BROTHERS TO PAY DUES. AS A RESULT, WE TRY TO KEEP OUR DUES AS LOW AS POSSIBLE. AFTER DUES TO THE IFC AND NATIONALS, AND PAYING FOR THE HOUSE, THERE ISN'T MUCH LEFT TO SPEND ON THE BROTHERHOOD. A PRESIDENT MUST KNOW HOW TO MOTIVATE MEMBERS TO RAISE FUNDS—EVEN THOUGH THAT IS THE LAST THING IN THE WORLD THEY WANT TO DO. THIS IS A HUGE, CONSTANT CHALLENGE IN OUR CHAPTER.

Brothers and sisters don't want to raise funds, but they want to enjoy the benefits of having extra money. They already have a ton of obligations their plates, and it's challenging to convince them to do something as painful as fund-raising activities.

The solution is to come up with fund-raising activities that require minimal time and effort but still have a significant enough payoff to make them worthwhile. There are literally hundreds. (I suggest more than twenty in my book, *The Fraternity Leader*.) But I strongly recommend you at least do the following two activities.

First, every chapter should conduct a fund-raising raffle each semester. This is the single easiest way for organizations to raise money quickly. (State governments do it with the lottery.)

Let's say your chapter is small and has only thirty members. Make it a requirement for every member to sell at least ten tickets at $10 each. This should raise a minimum of $3,000. Give the winner of the raffle whatever the hot item of the day is. When I wrote this advice, iPads were super popular. They cost about five hundred bucks. Hence, the chapter would net a quick $2,500 if it raffled off an iPad.

A great thing about raffles is that they have no up-front costs. You don't have to buy the iPad until the winner is chosen. There literally is no up-front investment.

Note that it doesn't matter who buys the tickets. Members can sell them to their friends, boyfriends, girlfriends, parents, dog, whomever…Every member should know at least ten people whom he or she can shame into dropping ten bucks for a ticket. And of course, members who are too lazy to sell raffle tickets can buy the tickets themselves. This is the most down-and-dirty fund-raising activity you can do, and I highly recommend it.

The second activity is a little more involved but it can have huge potential benefits. This is tapping into your alumni.

Most of your alumni donate to a myriad of different causes. Studies show that Greek alumni donate significantly more than their peers do. I donate varying amounts of money to roughly ten different causes. One of these causes is my fraternity. But I only give when they ask!

Of course, there has to be a strategy behind the request. If I got an e-mail out of the blue asking for money and hadn't heard from the chapter in forever, I'm probably not going to be terribly inclined to donate.

Here is what you would need to do to get me to donate:

First, write a short LETTER letting me know how the chapter is doing. Give me the facts that show me that the chapter is strong. Let me know how many members are in the undergraduate chapter. Tell me the size of the new member class. Tell me what the chapter GPA is, and how members are performing in intramurals. Share with me your big initiatives for the semester.

This letter doesn't have to be long — to be honest, short and sweet is better. I don't have the time or desire to read a long letter or newsletter, but I will gladly read a short one. Including pictures would be a great touch.

At the end of the letter, explain a specific need the chapter has. Then ask for a donation to pay for it.

Alumni are much more likely to give to a specific cause. We are also more prone to give if we see that the chapter is working to help itself. If you include a line stating that the chapter has already raised $XXX of its $X,XXX goal, then we are more eager to help.

Start out small with your request. The first semester, try to raise a couple hundred bucks for something you really need. Gradually increase the size of your request as your alumni base grows and brothers become accustomed to being asked to give.

Of course, make it easy on us to donate. Include a preaddressed, stamped envelope in which your alumni can send their checks. If I have to log on to PayPal or fish out an envelope, I am much more likely to wait until later—and then forget to do it.

Finally, be sure to thank your alumni who donate. Send a quick note letting each donor know that the fund-raiser was successful, and you sincerely appreciate his contribution.

Next semester when you ask again, lead the letter with a picture and story about what you purchased this semester. Also, publicly thank your alumni who contributed. With luck, the alumni who didn't contribute will feel the peer pressure and be more prone to donate in the future.

These two fund-raising activities must be done every semester, at a minimum. They generate easy money that the chapter can use to strengthen its operations budget.

Managing Money

Greek chapters are funny entities because young people with little or no accounting experience are given control of budgets of up to six-figure sums. My treasurer was someone I trusted but had bad money-management practices. He did things such as buying concerts tickets with chapter money and then trying to resell them to make a profit for the chapter. I believe his intentions were good, but he lost money for the chapter. I am not even sure that what he did was legal.

AS PRESIDENT, I USUALLY WAS TOO PREOCCUPIED WITH WHAT SEEMED TO BE MORE PRESSING MATTERS TO HAVE A SOLID UNDERSTANDING OF THE CHAPTER'S CASH FLOW. THIS MEMBER WAS LEFT UNCHECKED AND WAS RECKLESS WITH MONEY. MONEY MANAGEMENT CAN MAKE OR BREAK A CHAPTER.

A president and a chapter cannot be successful unless the finances are strong. As president, you have a responsibility to the organization to make sure the finances are handled professionally and appropriately.

If you take the following six steps, I can assure you that you will have a good grasp on the chapter's finances.

First, never deal in cash. Don't accept cash or pay for goods or services in cash. Make all financial transactions by check to ensure there is a paper trail. This will prove to be very valuable if there is ever a financial disagreement.

Second, every check that is paid by the chapter should require the signatures of the president and the treasurer. This will ensure that both the treasurer and the president know how every cent is being spent. Also, both people have to have the backbone to say no when they don't agree with the way money is being spent. Sometimes it is necessary for the president to block an expenditure, but he can't unless he knows how the money is being spent. Requiring two signatures also provides a check and balance to prevent fraudulent use of the chapter's money.

Third, the treasurer must present a weekly report of all expenses and collections. It is the president's job to verify these numbers by checking the bank statement online. It would be easy for a treasurer to phony up a statement to appease the membership. By having the president verify the information, it provides another check and balance that protects the chapter.

Fourth, the treasurer must report which members are delinquent in paying dues. The president needs to be informed because he can often help persuade members to pay their dues. Also, this puts a measure of peer pressure on delinquent members that should encourage them to honor their financial obligations.

Fifth, the chapter needs to have signed promissory notes from members who are delinquent on dues. This will guarantee that the chapter has legal grounds to collect, should the member become a complete deadbeat.

Sixth, the president and treasurer have to have a financial plan for the summer. Too often, chapters forget their financial obligations during the summer when dues money is not coming in. Be sure that the chapter is financially stable to make it through the long summer months.

If you follow these six tips, you will have a strong grasp on chapter finances and can make certain that the financial shenanigans that are too prevalent in today's society don't happen in your chapter.

Note that the treasurer may disagree with the need to do some of these things. You must explain that these processes aren't intended to keep the two of you honest; they are in place to ensure that everyone who serves in your positions in the future is honest. You might consider taking it a step further by adding these officer responsibilities to the bylaws of your chapter constitution. This will ensure that every president after you has the necessary backing to continue these very valuable practices.

Keeping Good Records

I DIDN'T REALIZE THE AMOUNT OF RECORD KEEPING INVOLVED IN BEING THE PRESIDENT OF MY CHAPTER. THE BEHIND-THE-SCENES STUFF TOOK AS MUCH TIME AS THE PUBLIC STUFF. IT IS ESSENTIAL FOR A PRESIDENT TO KEEP GOOD RECORDS AND ENSURE THAT IMPORTANT DOCUMENTS ARE MAINTAINED FOR FUTURE PRESIDENTS.

My mother told me that every mistake I make as an adult would cost me money. That has proven true in my life, and will prove true to you in your role as a chapter president. Let me share some examples.

When I was chapter president, we signed a lease with our landlord on a new house. As part of our lease, we had to put down $2,500 as a security deposit.

The chapter stayed in that house for a few years, and by the time we moved, I had long since graduated. However, when the chapter decided to move, the current president asked me for a copy of the lease. I told him that I'd given it to my successor. To make a long story short, no one could find the lease. The landlord held the only copy of the lease. Since we could not prove that the security deposit existed, the chapter never recovered that money.

The frequent leadership turnover in Greek chapters increases the chances that important documents will become lost. Therefore, it is imperative to send copies of important documents to your national headquarters as a backup. This way, they will always be available to the chapter.

Another example of the importance of keeping good records has to do with the chapter roll. When I became president, our roll with the university and our national headquarters included guys who were no longer in school. We had kicked some of them out of the fraternity because they weren't the high-quality men we wanted in our chapter. Others had graduated or left the university for a number of reasons. But our chapter was paying a significant amount of money to have them on our chapter roll. By making sure the roll was updated, we literally saved thousands of dollars—and we put that money to better use.

On top of that, some of the brothers we expelled were not good students. Their grade point averages were included in the chapter grade point average, since they were still on our chapter roll. Because we did not keep good records, we were hurting ourselves in one of the most important metrics on which a chapter is graded.

Brotherhood contracts are a third example. Our chapter had each brother sign a brotherhood contract that detailed his commitment to the chapter, including his promise to pay his dues. One brother, who was way behind on his dues, was expelled. The brotherhood wanted to go after him to collect the dues he owed, but we had lost the signed brotherhood contracts. Since we couldn't document the amount he owed, we were unable to collect the money.

Many chapter presidents assume that it is the chapter secretary's responsibility to keep track of these important documents. Of course it is. But it is also the duty of the chapter president to make sure the secretary is doing his job. If he isn't, it will cost the chapter money.

Make sure the secretary scans *all* important documents and send copies to HQ for safekeeping. This will take five minutes — arguably the best five minutes he spends in his leadership role.

A President's Responsibilities

What If the Chapter Resists Change?

> HOW SHOULD A PRESIDENT REACT WHEN THE CHAPTER IS RESISTANT TO CHANGE? DURING MY TERM, WE IMPLEMENTED A LOT OF NEW RULES AND TRADITIONS, AND WE DEFINITELY HAD TRADITIONALISTS IN THE CHAPTER WHO WERE OPPOSED TO WHAT WE WERE DOING. BEING ABLE TO TIE THOSE MEMBERS INTO OUR MISSION WOULD HAVE MADE OUR CHAPTER STRONGER, AND INNOVATION EASIER.

Chapters that have this problem go about implementing change the wrong way.

Look at it from the perspective of your membership. Members joined and love the chapter for what it is doing now. They probably don't understand why the leadership team wants to make changes. Or worse, they may think the changes are motivated by a power trip on the part of the president. If members think that's the case, they will buck any idea, regardless of how good it may be.

To overcome this problem, executive board members (especially the president) must convince chapter members to "buy in" before any change is proposed. Remember that good presidents know the result of every vote before that vote takes place.

To get members to back a proposal, the exec board needs to discuss it with individual members. They need to introduce the idea and get feedback from the membership. The purpose of these conversations is not to tell the member what is going to happen. The purpose is to get his or her opinion on the idea and solicit suggestions for making it better.

If you can do this, members will feel like they are part of the new idea. They will feel this way because it is true. Your members will now have "ownership" of the change, and will feel that it is partly their idea. People fight much harder when the idea is theirs.

If you do this extra legwork, you will find that in most cases, your members will be eager to accept change. In some cases, they will become the biggest advocates for the movement.

As president, there will be times when you have to get a tough vote passed. Sometimes the right side of that vote will not be popular. If you can make members understand why the change must happen, your chapter will be stronger, and innovation will come easier.

WHAT DOES YOUR CHAPTER WANT?

A PRESIDENT SHOULD KNOW HOW TO MOTIVATE MEMBERS AND HOW TO MAXIMIZE DATA HE CAN GET FROM THEM TO BUILD A GREAT YEAR FOR THE GENERAL MEMBERSHIP. OUR CHAPTER USED WWW.SURVEYMONKEY. COM TO GATHER INFORMATION FROM THE MEMBERSHIP TO SEE HOW MANY EVENTS WE SHOULD HAVE AND HOW IMPORTANT ONE TYPE OF EVENT WAS OVER ANOTHER. WE ALSO GOT FEEDBACK ABOUT CHANGES IN THE COMING YEAR. WE GOT GREAT PIECES OF DATA THAT REALLY HELPED MY EXECUTIVE BOARD SET GOALS AND STRETCH GOALS FOR THE CHAPTER FOR THE SEMESTER.

This is a brilliant strategy. As chapter president, your role is to serve your membership, not the other way around. This means doing what your members want, not necessarily what you want.

You can give them what they want by finding out what they want. You may think you have a good feel for this already, and maybe you do. But doesn't it make sense to ask the members what they want to remove any doubt?

Start by giving an anonymous survey. This is super easy and takes no time to do. Ask the members what the chapter does well and what the chapter does poorly. Ask where they see room for improvement. Ask what types of events they want to see the chapter have. This type of information is gold for a leader.

Then talk about the survey results. Send the results to every member. This isn't a state secret. It is a great tool with which to start conversations on how to improve the chapter. If you do this, a couple things will happen as a result.

The membership will become more motivated because the chapter will actually be doing what the members want. People will always be more motivated to see their own ideas become successful.

They will also appreciate that the leadership team actually took their recommendations to heart. This will create a happier chapter.

The members will become much more engaged with each other. They will talk about the results of the survey and have conversations about what the chapter needs to do to improve. This is extremely healthy. It's a sure sign of a chapter that is on the cusp of dramatic improvement.

Take five minutes and send a survey out. Let the membership know that you are eager to learn what they want and make their vision of the chapter become a reality. This could be the best move you make as chapter president.

Improving Academics

> MY CHAPTER HAS HAD MANY ISSUES WITH HOLDING MEMBERS ACCOUNTABLE TO A GRADE-POINT-AVERAGE MINIMUM. IT OFTEN GETS PERSONAL WHEN PEOPLE DON'T WANT TO GET RID OF SOMEONE WHO DIDN'T PERFORM WELL ACADEMICALLY, BUT IT IS MORE IMPORTANT TO UPHOLD FAIR RULES FOR EVERYONE. THE PRESIDENT MUST BE ABLE TO FIGURE OUT HOW TO STRESS ACADEMICS IN THE CHAPTER.

I won many awards during my time as an undergraduate. I think the biggest accomplishment that I had in the eyes of the selection committees was that my chapter's GPA increased all four semesters that I was chapter president. This metric really mattered to them, and I was rewarded as a result.

Most advisers will tell you to increase your chapter GPA by recruiting higher-caliber students. That is almost as helpful as someone telling you that you need to go to class and study to get better grades. No kidding, right?

Fortunately, there are other ways to improve your chapter GPA. Here are nine steps I followed as chapter president that greatly helped me improve my chapter's GPA. I highly recommend them to any chapter president.

Step 1: Our GPA mattered to me. I knew this was a tangible metric that I could use to evaluate my success as a leader and our improvement as a chapter. I also knew that many members, if not most, did not care about it. They only cared about their own academic achievement. I let other members know it was important to me in the hope that it would become more important to them.

Step 2: I made sure our chapter roster was accurate. When I became chapter president, the chapter roster was not up to date and included a bunch of people who were no longer in the chapter. Most of these former members were poor students and were dragging down our chapter GPA. Removing these individuals from our roster had a dramatic impact on our chapter GPA.

Step 3: I took care of the new-member class. If you overburden the new-member class, the members will not have time to study. If you keep them up all night, they will not go to class. I am all for challenging them and having them prove that they are worthy of membership. But doing so at the expense of academics is like cutting your leg off to lose weight.

Step 4: I organized study sessions for younger members and new members. At my school, freshman and sophomores took classes that had standardized midterm and final exams. I would recruit an older member who was proficient in that subject to hold study sessions before tests for the younger members. The older member understood the material and from experience knew what was

24

probably going to be asked on the tests. These study sessions significantly helped the younger members learn the material.

Step 5: I encouraged every member to take one "fluff" class per semester to get an easy A. This was huge for people like me. I was an electrical engineering major, and most of my classes were way over my head. But I made sure to take one freshman-level class each semester to get an easy A. This class did nothing to meet my graduation requirements, but it was huge for my GPA. Roughly one-sixth of my total college GPA can be credited to these classes. For the rest of my life, people will think I was a good student because of my GPA. Little do they know how my GPA was inflated…

Step 6: I took classes with members and encouraged other members to do the same. This was a great way to hold each other accountable for going to class. We also studied together and shared notes. We all had a stake in each others' success. As a result, we all succeeded. On top of that, we all became closer friends because of the time we spent together.

Step 7: I did my very best to balance academic and chapter scheduling. I tried to minimize chapter functions on Thursdays. I knew this was a big party night in college, but I also knew that members had class on Friday. I tried to avoid planning chapter functions (initiation, big parties, and formals) around popular test times. This was very easy to figure out because I was able to see when the majority of the exams were scheduled for my classes. I figured if I had exams, then others did too.

Step 8: I avoided using punishment to improve chapter GPA. I don't think mandatory study halls work. It wasn't my place to tell another grown person when he should or shouldn't study. I did not impose punishments for failure to meet a certain GPA. I felt that this was difficult to administer because not all curriculums or semesters are equal. In addition, the university has standards that a student must meet to remain enrolled and to graduate.

Step 9: We made sure that our GPA was public knowledge, and that excellence was recognized. The chapter recognized members who worked their tails off to succeed in the classroom. The members who didn't work hard and were holding the chapter back could no longer hide in anonymity. Everyone knew were everyone stood, and the entire chapter could look after the members who were struggling in school.

As the president of your chapter, you are charged with taking care of your organization. You cannot have a healthy chapter unless your members are succeeding academically. Foster an environment where academic achievement is stressed and valued. If you chapter is succeeding academically, I promise you that you will achieve in other areas as well.

Improving Your Chapter's Image

PUBLIC RELATIONS ARE A HUGE PROBLEM FOR OUR CHAPTER. OUR MEMBERS ARE VERY CONCERNED WITH OUR IMAGE ON CAMPUS BUT DON'T KNOW WHAT TO DO TO BE SEEN IN A POSITIVE LIGHT. THIS IS SOMETHING THAT EVERY CHAPTER PRESIDENT WILL HAVE TO ADDRESS.

This is an important issue in the eyes of many presidents. They desperately want to improve the image of the chapter but don't know where to start.

Some presidents believe that a huge community-service project is the answer. These presidents will convince the chapter that this is the best way to "get our name out there" and will commit the members to something they don't want to do.

The president will have a hell of a hard time getting members to participate, and the event will not have the desired outcome because the members' hearts are only half in it. On top of that, any

27

positive press received from the event is short-lived, as people will quickly forget about it.

There is a better way. Outsiders' impressions of a chapter are created through the opinions they have of individual members. Put yourself in the shoes of your professors. They don't know chapter 123 from chapter XYZ, and they really don't care. But if they are particularly fond of a student whom they know belongs to chapter 123, then they will probably assume that the chapter is OK too.

If you are a fraternity guy, think about it from the perspective of a sorority sister. This sister is not going to know a lot about your chapter, but she will probably know a few of your members. If she thinks highly of those members, then chances are she will think highly of the chapter. This obviously works in reverse too.

Because peoples' opinion of the chapter will be based on their opinions of individual members, it is imperative that your individual members are held in high regard. So how does a chapter president make sure this happens?

First, you need to recruit high-caliber people. An important litmus test is whether you would want the opinion of this person to become the opinion others have of you. If you aren't comfortable with this person representing you around campus, then you probably should pass on recruiting him.

Second, we must hold each other accountable and take care of each other. Greeks do dumb things. All college students do. If a member is doing something that will reflect poorly on her or the chapter, it is critical that her sisters remove her from that situation. It only takes one bad action to ruin the reputation of the entire chapter.

Third, members need to be presentable. If a member rolls out of bed and goes to class in sweats without brushing her teeth, she will make a poor impression on her professor and classmates. If a member attends a function wearing clothes that look like they were dug from the bottom of his dirty-clothes hamper, that will make an impression on everyone in attendance. And these impressions become the impression of the entire chapter.

Fourth, members need to be proud of their chapter and make sure others know it. If you are a high-caliber individual but no one knows you are a member of your chapter, then it doesn't do the chapter much good. Wear your letters and be proud of them.

Fifth, have exemplary manners. For men, this means that when a woman enters the room, stand up. When a woman leaves the table, stand up. Hold doors open. Don't swear. It only takes one small act for a woman to label you a gentleman. For women, always show class and grace. Avoid gossiping. Avoid being pretentious. Be pleasant and approachable. These little things will color what others think of you, and that will become the image they have of your chapter.

Sixth, recover in a world-class way. People will make mistakes. How you respond to those mistakes will affect what people think of you. People have an amazing capacity to forgive. If you take the high road by owning up to your mistakes, making the necessary corrections and apologies, and then moving on, people will think very highly of you.

Seventh, help others. Community-service projects are great, and they are the responsibility of the more fortunate. If you really want to create goodwill though, help others with *their* community-service endeavors. The benefit is that the entire organization will recognize that your chapter is helping their cause and helping to make them look better. They will be grateful and have a great opinion of you in return.

Eighth, talk about chapter membership with those who don't understand it. When someone from the "buying your friends" crowd starts talking poorly about Greek life, calmly discuss what you get out of your membership. When a professor makes a negative comment about Greek life, explain to her why you are a member of your chapter. Part of being a member of your chapter is being an ambassador for all Greeks.

Finally, as a chapter president, you set the tone for the entire organization. Other members, especially the younger ones, will be looking at your example. In a way, the image you present will become the image of the chapter because you will become the most widely recognized member. When you were elected, you accepted the challenge and opportunity of being the face of the chapter. Be the type of leader that your members are proud to have representing them.

If you and your members can do these things, then people with whom you interact will think highly of you. Those individual opinions will become the public image of the chapter.

How to Groom the Next Leaders

I am the president of my chapter. I am fearful about the lack of leadership I see in our younger members. What do I need to do to groom the next batch of leaders so my chapter continues to improve once I'm gone?

A leader always has to have an eye to the future. All the great things you are accomplishing now will mean very little once you are gone if your successor is not a good leader.

So what steps can you take to groom the future leaders of your chapter?

The most crucial thing you can do is identify the younger members of the chapter who show leadership ability and the desire to be involved. You need to find both qualities. One without the other is a recipe for trouble.

Once you have identified these members, you must give them the opportunity to grow as leaders. The best way to do this is to make them responsible for something. Put them in charge of planning an event. Put them in charge of a chapter responsibility, such as managing the athletic program or the house. If they are responsible for something, you and others have an opportunity to mentor them.

Once a potential leader has a task, sit down with him or her and talk about it. Don't dominate the conversation. Part of the grooming process is letting these members figure things out on their own. Don't take this important step away from them. Your role is to stress the importance of what they are doing, and communicate that the chapter hopes the task is a stepping-stone to more responsibility. And then listen to the ideas they have. You may be very impressed by what you hear.

Part of this process is giving potential leaders guidance on where to go for advice. Let them know to whom on your campus they can go for suggestions. Let them know what resources are out there (shameless plug: my books and www.thefraternityadvisor. com) and encourage them to learn.

Of course, you need to stress that you are always there to support them so they can be successful. They need to know that they can count on you whenever they need assistance.

When the task is accomplished, sit down with the member and evaluate how he or she did. Offer tips on what could have been done better. Always encourage and praise what was done well. And never forget to thank the member for all his or her hard work.

Finally, be sure to give the member another responsibility and start the process over again. You will see improvement, and the chapter will be better for it.

One of the best parts of this process is it will make you a more effective president. Instead of getting lost in the day-to-day tasks of running a chapter, you will be taking a strategic role and managing the organization. You will be grooming future leaders while having a direct role in your current success.

Let me share a little secret: If you follow this process, you will learn how to better manage relationships and motivate others to perform. In short, you will be training yourself to become a better leader.

Do the Right Thing

WE HAD A SITUATION ABOUT A YEAR AGO
WHEN POLICE GOT A WARRANT TO SEARCH
OUR HOUSE AND FOUND THOUSANDS OF
DOLLARS WORTH OF STOLEN GOODS FROM
PLEDGE CLASSES PAST. THEY CHARGED US
WITH GRAND LARCENY. (THE CHARGES WERE
EVENTUALLY DROPPED.) OBVIOUSLY, THE
FIRST THING WE DID WAS CALL OUR CHAPTER
ADVISER AND THEN OUR PROVINCE ARCHON.
THEY IMMEDIATELY GOT A HOLD OF OUR
NATIONAL LAWYER. THE MOST IMPORTANT
THING IS TO TELL THE TRUTH, ESPECIALLY TO
THE LAWYERS. THEY ARE THERE TO HELP YOU,
AND IF YOU DO NOT TELL THE TRUTH, THEN
YOU ARE PROBABLY GOING TO BE KICKED OFF
CAMPUS OR WORSE.

Your chapter will screw up during your time as president. It is
inevitable that someone will do something stupid. It is always

better to take the high road and come clean rather than try to cover it up.

My chapter had an incident several years ago when it planned a formal at the beach. Chapter members located a few houses that were next to each other and planned for a great time.

There was one slight problem, though. The rental agreements specifically said the houses were not to be rented to fraternities. So, a brother served as the front man and rented the houses under his name.

During one night of the formal, a few brothers got stupid and started chucking furniture off the balcony. I believe they were aiming for the pool, but I can't say for sure. Needless to say, damage was done to the property.

They paid for the damage promptly, and the chapter thought the problem had gone away. However, the ruse of having a brother sign for the houses was about to be exposed.

The owner of the house was not happy. He started investigating the situation. He obviously knew the brother who rented the house, so he checked out that brother's Facebook page. Naturally, there were dozens of pictures showing the crazy time they had at the formal.

The owner was now pissed that they had lied to him and reported the incident to the university. When the chapter president was confronted, he lied to the university about what had happened. He maintained his false story for a few days before he finally came clean. Because of the president's poor judgment, the chapter was punished with social probation for a semester.

The thing was, there really wasn't much to cover up. Sure, the chapter lied on the rental application, but it made good on the rental payment and paid for all damage. If the president had been truthful when asked about the situation, the chapter would not have received more than a slap on the wrist. Instead, deceit turned a nonissue into a big issue.

When I was chapter president, we screwed up too. A new member drank excessively and showed up for a chapter function extremely intoxicated. He passed out and hit his head on the porch. To make a long story short, we had to take this eighteen-year-old new member to the hospital that night to be treated for alcohol poisoning.

We stayed there all night with him. First thing the next day, I called our Greek life director and reported what had happened. I also explained what the chapter was going to do in the future to ensure this problem would not happen again.

To my amazement, we were not punished because of that incident. We were actually commended for being responsible because we got the new member the help he needed.

When your chapter screws up, be sure to take control of the situation. That means owning up to your mistakes. Remember, it is always better for the Greek life office to find out about problems in your chapter from you, rather than from other sources.

If the situation requires you to report yourself, be sure you are equipped with a clear understanding of why the incident occurred and what you are going to do in the future to ensure it doesn't happen again. Being equipped with a solution to lapses in the risk-management program shows maturity and strength in your leadership. Always strive to be part of the solution.

Taking the high road will ensure the longevity of your chapter. It will let outsiders know that you are men of high integrity, and that is something that is valued.

The Importance of Your Ritual

RITUAL IS ALWAYS KEY. THAT IS THE EMBODIMENT OF WHAT WE ARE AND HOW WE EXIST. EVERY SORORITY OR FRATERNITY HAS A RITUAL AND A SET OF IDEALS THAT MAKE THEM WHO THEY ARE. EVERY DECISION SHOULD BE BASED ON THESE IDEALS. IF SOMETHING DOESN'T COINCIDE WITH WHAT YOUR ORGANIZATION'S IDEALS ARE, DON'T DO IT.

Ritual is commonly misunderstood.

Your ritual is not the event you hold when you bring new members into your chapter. That is your initiation ceremony. Your ritual is a very important part of that ceremony, but it is much more significant than the proceedings of just that one night.

The ritual is the set of values and ideals that members are supposed to follow every day. The ritual is part of our heritage and tradition. It is what makes us different from the other organizations on campus. It is our guide to becoming better people. As president, you play a key role in making sure your organization lives up to your ritual.

The president needs to make sure that his or her members understand the values that form the basis of the ritual. One of the most important things you can do as president is to sit down with the new members after initiation and go through the ritual with them. These values will not be a secret to your newest members at this stage of their Greek experience, but it is important to take the time to explain the ritual, as it forms the foundation of the entire organization. When you conduct this ritual review, be sure that all members are invited. There is no reason why others cannot participate in celebrating such an important part of your organization.

The president also must make sure members live up to the expectations of the ritual in the way they conduct themselves. The ritual can serve as a guide of what the chapter should and should not do. When the chapter finds itself in a situation that does not fit the values of the organization, then the president needs to have the courage to get the chapter back on track. This duty does not rest solely with the president, though. All members should have the confidence to do what is right because they know the ritual supports their actions.

Another common misconception is that your ritual is a secret. Your ritual ceremony absolutely should be kept a secret. Secrecy is one of the aspects that makes traditions special.

But everyone you associate with should be able to tell that the values of your ritual are important to you. Your values are not a secret. People should see that you value scholarship, leadership, service, religion, fellowship, or any of the other great virtues that are important to Greeks. This is what makes us different. This is what makes our organizations great.

As president, be sure you understand the ritual and make a point to live it. Make sure the ritual is reflected in the actions of your members and the events of your chapter. Teach others the ritual, and encourage them to make the lessons of your founders an important part of their lives. If you do, you will have a strong chapter that will encourage growth in your members.

Managing the Chapter Meeting

Our chapter meetings are awful. They last for hours and seem pointless. The most frustrating part is the group that sits in the corner and complains about everything that this being discussed. A chapter president definitely needs to know how to manage a meeting.

If your members dread the chapter meeting, then you are doing it wrong. Chances are if your meetings are awful, you have turned them into unguided debate sessions instead of planned information sessions. Well-run organizations never let this happen.

The purpose of your meeting is to disseminate information and vote on key issues. The meeting should be designed to increase the goodwill of the chapter. Everything else will just pollute the meeting and should not be included.

There are two parts to a chapter meeting, the preparation and the execution. I will break down both parts.

The preparation: As president, you need to know the rules of the chapter. This is the code you have to follow when leading your meetings. These rules are your chapter constitution and bylaws. Read them and understand them.

You also need to decide where and when to have the meeting. The meeting should always be held at a time when most members can attend. It makes the most sense to me to hold them on Sunday evenings because there is no fear of class interference. Obviously, however, that is a decision you will have to make.

The meeting should be held at a location that can comfortably hold the entire chapter. In most cases, a classroom on campus would make sense if you don't have enough room at the chapter house. If you want a professional meeting, you need to have it in a professional setting.

You also will have to decide how often to have meetings. Most chapters elect to have a weekly meeting. If your chapter is comfortable with that schedule, then keep it. However, I believe the weekly meeting tradition is a holdover from the pre-Internet days and is not necessary. Information can be disseminated electronically to keep the entire membership abreast of the happenings of the chapter.

The most critical portion of the preparation is the executive board meeting. This is where chapter strategy is developed and monitored. This is where the performance of the committees is evaluated. Many of the discussions that chapters with bad meetings complain about should take place in the executive board meeting or in committee meetings — not in the general meeting. When the executive board makes a decision, the executive board members must be unified in supporting it in front of the chapter.

Finally, an agenda needs to be prepared for the meeting. It should consist of officer reports, committee reports, new business, and old business. This should provide the necessary structure to ensure a smooth meeting.

The meeting: The actual meeting must have a set start time and end time. Begin the meeting exactly at the start time out of respect to those who showed up on time. Do not repeat information for those who come late. It is the job of the president to make sure that meeting does not run past the stated end time.

Again, realize that the meeting is primarily an information session. As such, don't let the brothers or sisters debate decisions during the chapter meeting. Calmly suggest that they speak to the committee chairperson after the meeting. The debates should take place in committee meetings. That is their purpose.

The one exception to this rule is when a chapter vote is required. Most commonly, this involves voting on new members. While discussion is inevitable before these votes, do not let it drag on. The second you feel the members have made up their minds, call a quick vote to see if anyone wants further discussion on the topic. Often, no one does, and you can take the vote. This little trick eliminates a lot of pointless debate.

There are several key components to every meeting:

First is the president's report. The most important part of this report is giving public recognition to those who deserve it. Thank and recognize members who achieve. It motivates other members to achieve.

Second is the treasurer's report. I discuss this topic in the chapter on how to collect dues, but I'll reiterate it here because it is very important. The entire chapter needs to know the status of chapter finances. I cannot stress that enough.

Third are committee reports. It is obvious that members need to know what is happening and when. A key component to committee reports is drumming up support for the chapter's activities. As president, you need to explain that to the committee heads. This is where your leadership can have a direct impact on the morale of the chapter.

Fourth is a chapter adviser's report. Often, the chapter adviser will serve as a cheerleader if things are going well. If they aren't, the adviser can provide advice on how to improve. Strong chapters have active chapter advisers.

Finally, there should be a "for the good and welfare of the chapter" component to the meeting. This is when members can make announcements that are outside the formal structure of a fraternity or sorority. This can add a great deal of fun to the meeting.

If you follow this strategy, your chapter meetings will productive and well attended.

You are Not a One-Man Wolfpack

SOME PRESIDENTS TRY TO DO THE WORK OF THE ENTIRE CHAPTER. IF HE DOES IT ALONE, HE GETS BURNED OUT AND EVERYTHING CRASHES. A PRESIDENT MUST LEARN TO PACE HIMSELF TO MAKE SURE HE MAKES IT THROUGH HIS TERM.

A leader whom I really respect explained to me that one of the most important things a leader must realize is that he must have his life in balance. For Greek presidents, this means balancing school, personal life, and Greek commitments.

This is tough. It probably seems tougher after reading this book. But you have to realize that you cannot be everything to everybody, and your life must be in balance if you are to succeed as president.

This means that you cannot neglect to take care of yourself. You need to attempt to eat healthy meals and exercise. You need to avoid binge drinking when you finally feel like you can let your hair down. You need to make sure you are in a good place mentally. If you aren't, it will show up in your attitude, and you will not be an effective leader.

You also need to make sure you manage your academics. In my first semester as chapter president, I made a 2.0—straight Cs. I was so excited about finally being president that I neglected my academic responsibilities. The problem was that this was a critical semester for me academically. I was just getting into the core classes for my major, and the rest of my academic career built on what I was supposed to have learned that semester. This made the rest of college a struggle for me, as I did not have a good foundation in the core classes. Don't make the same mistake I did.

The only way you will be able to keep your life in balance is if you delegate some chores and remain organized.

When you delegate, be sure the person you are working with has a clear understanding of your expectations and the desired outcome of the project. Be sure to ask her if she needs any resources to achieve this desired outcome. Then get out of the way. You have trusted her to do a good job. Let her do it.

Of course, eventually you will need to follow up and get an update. With everything going on in the chapter, this could mean doing a ton of follow-ups. As a result, it is essential that you keep an organized task list of everything you have delegated. Don't forget that you can delegate the follow-ups to a trusted person too.

Being organized goes much deeper than that, though, and it is an essential time-management tool. With everything you will have on your plate, you need to be sure you don't let things slip through the cracks. Every mistake you make will cost you or your chapter, and you can't afford to let things drop.

Military officer training is essentially the same type of time-management challenge. It isn't the physical part of military training that is grueling; it is the mental part. The military believes that to test aspiring leaders, you need to give them more tasks to do in a day than they can possibly accomplish. A good leader can quickly prioritize what is important and make sure these critical tasks are addressed. Inevitably, some of the less important tasks will not be completed, and that is OK. The key is making sure you prioritize correctly. This is the exact same challenge a Greek president will face.

There is no doubt that being chapter president is a daunting responsibility. It is a time-management nightmare that can swamp even the most prepared leaders. Realize, though, that it is OK to check out in order to maintain your balance. Maybe you need to lay low on a weekend or two to catch up on sleep. Maybe you have to miss a weeknight function or two to make sure you are keeping your grades up. It is OK and understandable. No one can do everything. Not even the president.

COMMUNICATION

I THINK ONE OF THE MOST DIFFICULT DAY-TO-DAY SITUATIONS IS COMMUNICATION. INSTANT COMMUNICATION DOES NOT NECESSARILY MAKE THINGS MORE CLEAR AND CAN LEAD TO MISUNDERSTANDINGS THAT CAN FESTER AND CAUSE INTER-CHAPTER CONFLICT. COMMITTEE DISCUSSIONS OR MEETINGS SHOULD NOT BE HELD VIA TEXT OR FACEBOOK MESSAGING.

I am going to take this opportunity to rant…

The cell phone generation frustrates the hell out of me. It is rude to have your phone on the table and to check it twenty times during a meal. It is ruder to text when you are having a conversation with someone. It is ruder still to take a call in the middle of a conversation. When you do these types of things, you are essentially telling the person you are with that the person on the other end of the phone is more important. This shows poor manners.

The cell phone is a wonderful tool, but it has taken the place of real human interaction. It is crippling an entire generation's ability to communicate.

At this point, you have read a good portion of this book. Note that in nearly every topic I have discussed, the solution is to have real, face-to-face conversations with others to resolve issues. Many problems can't be worked out via text or FB messaging.

A big part of your role as president is to communicate your chapter's vision and plans. You can only succeed at communicating a vision by having real conversations with your members. This is the only way to get members to buy in. Conversations give members the opportunity to ask questions and voice their concerns. It also shows them that you genuinely care about their opinions. Conversations give you the opportunity to explain the vision completely, leaving nothing open to interpretation. You get to share the excitement you have, and excitement is infectious.

Communicating plans is easier face-to-face. E-mail, mass texts, FB, and other platforms are all great ways to spread key information about the chapter. There is simply no reason that a member should ever feel left out or feel uniformed with the tools that a chapter has at its disposal. Make sure that when you use these communication media you make your message clear and concise. People don't read; they skim. If you send a message that is too long, they will often miss the important information. Keep your communications short and sweet when you are sharing information. Less is definitely more. If you need to send more, then that is when you need to talk.

You should note that as president, you don't literally have to be the individual who makes all chapter communications. This is impractical and ineffective. You do have responsibility to make sure that someone is doing it, though. You also have the responsibility to guide and coach those who are not communicating properly.

A huge part of leadership depends on your ability to communicate. If you hide behind a touch screen or computer monitor, then you cannot be a good leader. Be sure to engage your membership in real conversations. Be sure to encourage others to do the same. You will find that this will improve your chapter.

CONFLICT MEDIATION

BEING A CONFLICT MEDIATOR IS A HUGE
ROLE OF A CHAPTER PRESIDENT. DURING MY
TERM AS PRESIDENT, I HAD A PARTICULARLY
MESSY INCIDENT BETWEEN TWO MEMBERS.
THESE MEMBERS DISAGREED WITH HOW
THE FORMAL WAS BEING PLANNED, AND
THE DISAGREEMENT QUICKLY BECAME
PERSONAL. A PRESIDENT NEEDS TO KNOW
HOW TO MEDIATE ISSUES BETWEEN MEMBERS
SO SMALL PROBLEMS DON'T BECOME BIG
PROBLEMS.

Conflict mediation is not fun at all. Not one wants to be in the middle of an ugly squabble between friends. However, as chapter president, it is often your duty to step in and help resolve issues.

First, you must realize when it is your role to step in. If the problem is affecting the chapter, then it is proper for you to step in. If it is a personal disagreement between members, be very careful that you don't overstep your bounds.

If it is proper to get involved, your objective is to get the two parties together to discuss the issue as soon as possible. Conflict has a way of growing over time, and it is easiest to solve in its infancy.

The mediation should always be done at a neutral site. You don't want either party to feel like she is at a disadvantage in the discussion. Your role as mediator is very clear. You are there to help facilitate a conversation that will lead to a resolution that pleases both sides. At the conclusion of the discussion, both sides need to feel that they have won something.

You are not there to solve the problem or pass judgment on either side. The moment that one of combatants suspects you are playing favorites, you have failed as a mediator. You need to remain impartial with the one goal of helping two people solve their own problem.

It is also important that you always keep the problem and the people separate. You are trying to help guide them to a solution to a problem. As a mediator, you cannot let it get personal.

Here are a few tricks to help steer the conversation toward resolution.

1. Keep the conversation on point. When one or both parties starts talking in circles, you can summarize their points and steer the conversation in a healthy direction.

2. Make sure the conversation is not confrontational. You can do this by stressing the goal of the conversation — to make sure both sides are happy with the resolution. Asking each participant what it would take to resolve the issue is a good way to keep the conversation productive.

3. You need to remain positive and encouraging. The individuals going through the conflict are in the middle of a

stressful situation. They probably don't want to be there, and the meeting can quickly go downhill if you cannot keep it positive.

4. Make sure emotions are kept in check. Set ground rules that neither party can get angry or blame the other party for what happened. Everyone is going to focus on the facts of what happened and work together to find a resolution. You cannot properly mediate if people are angry or emotional. It is important that you keep both parties in line.

5. Finally, realize that it is OK for the parties to disagree as long as both acknowledge and understand why there is a disagreement. A potential outcome may be to find mutual understanding. Sometimes parties simply have to understand their differences.

Being a conflict mediator is tough. It is definitely one of the thankless jobs of a chapter president. However, it is essential to keeping members happy with each other. And the happier your membership is, the better the chapter will be.

DEALING WITH OUTSIDERS

A CHAPTER PRESIDENT NEEDS TO KNOW HOW TO DEAL WITH CAMPUS OFFICIALS, LOCAL VOLUNTEER ADVISERS, REGIONAL ADVISERS, NATIONAL-LEVEL ADVISERS, ETC. A DISCUSSION OF HOW TO BUILD RAPPORT WITH POLICE, FIRE FIGHTERS, CITY OFFICIALS, SCHOOL OFFICIALS, AND NEIGHBORS WOULD BE GREAT. PR FOR GREEKS IS TOO OFTEN ABOUT WORKING WITH OTHER GREEKS. WHILE THIS IS IMPORTANT, IT REALLY IS THE EASIEST PART OF THE JOB.

Being the face of the organization is another of the Greek president's key roles. The most important aspect of this role is developing relationships with key outsiders *before* something happens.

Too often, we meet the director of student conduct after the chapter gets in trouble. Too often, we only find out how our neighbors feel about us after they call the cops to shut down one of our parties. Too often, we meet our executive director when we need her help.

It would be so much smarter to meet these key people before you are forced to meet them. For example, let's say your chapter house is off campus in a residential neighborhood. Wouldn't it be smart to meet and develop relationships with your neighbors? If you are a good neighbor, they will be more willing to tolerate the antics of college kids.

This is especially smart before an event at the house. Talk with your neighbors. Let them know your plans. Tell them to call your cell phone if they have any problems. This beats having them call the cops.

It is smart to meet the folks at the office of student conduct as well. If your chapter gets in trouble, this staff more than likely will administer the investigation and sanctions. When you introduce yourself, ask for advice on how to make sure your chapter abides by university policies. Ask what situations typically get chapters in trouble, and ask for advice on avoiding these situations.

Having the exact same conversation with your volunteer alumni/alumnae and national headquarters. In addition to the risk-management conversation, ask questions about how to make your chapter the best it can be.

There are many reasons why developing relationships with key people in your community is smart. Learning from these folks will make you a better leader and more prepared to lead your chapter. It also might open the door to advantages for you and your chapter because they'll remember you when unique opportunities come up. Finally, if your chapter gets into trouble, these people will be more apt to assist if their first impression of you was positive.

Take the time and meet the key people in your community. It's a worthwhile investment and will make you a better Greek president.

DEALING WITH THE ALUM ASSOCIATION AND HOUSING CORPORATION

OUR ALUMNI ASSOCIATION ALWAYS FELT LIKE OUR PARENTS. WE WOULD GO TO THEM WHEN WE NEEDED MONEY OR MESSED UP. THEY HAD TO BAIL US OUT, OR AT LEAST THAT'S THE WAY PREVIOUS PRESIDENTS HAD HANDLED SITUATIONS. THIS OFTEN CAUSED THEM TO WORRY ABOUT THE GENERAL CONDITION OF THE CHAPTER. THEY WOULD COME TO OUR CHAPTER MEETINGS AND TELL US HOW TERRIBLE WE WERE DOING OR LECTURE US. THIS BUILT UP A HUGE RESENTMENT BETWEEN OUR ACTIVES AND OUR ALUMNI, WHICH WAS VERY NEGATIVE. A PRESIDENT REALLY NEEDS TO UNDERSTAND HOW TO FOSTER GOOD RELATIONSHIPS WITH THE ALUMNI.

Most of your alumni/alumnae will completely check out of the chapter once they graduate from college. Other things take priority in their lives, and the fraternity or sorority gets pushed aside. That is not to say that these Greeks stop caring, however. Most will always care, but they will do so from a passive mindset.

On the other hand, some alumni/alumnae choose to remain active. These alums are like gold for your chapter. They eagerly give back and can be key allies for you as president. It is essential that you keep both groups happy. You keep them happy by doing three things:

1. Meet with them at the beginning of the school year and learn what their expectations are. Some will be obvious. For example, the housing corporation will expect you to pay on time. Other expectations may not be obvious. You need to know what they are so you can plan to meet them.
2. Develop relationships with your active alumni/alumnae. You don't have to do anything elaborate. Just make sure you know them and they know you. This is a great time to get advice on how to improve your chapter. Meeting them early in your term will pay huge dividends down the road, should you ever need them to help you get out of a pickle.
3. Make sure the alumni/alumnae are kept aware of what is happening in the chapter. Put a reminder on your iPhone to send a mass e-mail to your alums once a month to give updates on the chapter. You don't have to write it; in fact, it's probably better to have a dedicated alumni/alumnae chairperson write it. But you should be the one who sends it. They will want to know how the chapter is doing in recruitment. They will want to know how the chapter is faring athletically and academically. They will want to know

about any social or community service functions that are taking place. (Be sure to send an open invite to any event that seems appropriate.) They will want to know about any challenges the chapter is facing. They will want to know any interesting news from other alumni. Don't forget to include a couple of good pictures. The goal of these e-mails is to let alums know that you care about them and that the chapter is doing well. This can do nothing but strengthen the relationship you have with your predecessors. This e-mail does not have to be long. In fact, short and sweet is best. It should take no longer than twenty minutes to knock out once a month.

If you reach out to your alumni/alumnae in these ways, they will feel like they are still part of the chapter and they will not treat you like kids. However, if you avoid them and only reach out to them when you desperately need help, then you know what to expect. Keep your alumni active and involved. It's a sign of a strong chapter.

GUIDE TO PUBLIC SPEAKING

THE CHAPTER PRESIDENT WILL HAVE TO DO
A FAIR AMOUNT OF PUBLIC SPEAKING. THIS
WAS SOMETHING I ALWAYS DREADED AND
WAS NOT VERY GOOD AT. PUBLIC SPEAKING IS
DEFINITELY SOMETHING THAT FUTURE CHAPTER
PRESIDENTS SHOULD BE PREPARED FOR.

As president of the fraternity or sorority, you will do more than
your fair share of public speaking. Many presidents think this is
their platform to let others know how brilliant they are. They are
full of confidence and relish the opportunity. An equal number
don't take this responsibility seriously and end up winging it.
They figure that they are smart enough to think on the fly. Some
fraternity presidents neglect this responsibility completely. They
don't like to talk in front of others, don't see the point, and avoid
it. Many fraternity presidents—those who speak willingly and
those for whom it is a chore—are not polished in their delivery

of public remarks, and the umms and uhhhs detract from their message.

Don't fall into these public speaking traps! As the leader of the chapter, you are charged with presenting messages to the membership on frequent occasions. You should always speak to the members during big events, such as your formal and graduation ceremonies.

My advice is to keep it brief. Always thank everyone for coming, and say a quick thing or two about the event or the person being honored. Finally, and most importantly, thank those who worked hard to plan the event. You must always publically recognize the folks who do the work for the chapter.

I'll let you in on a secret: the thank you is the only part anyone will ever remember. And the only person who will remember it is the person being thanked. Think about the times your current chapter president spoke in the past year. Can you remember anything she said? You probably can't unless she made some type of major gaffe. Therefore, keep your addresses short, sweet, and filled with thank-yous.

A couple more dos and don'ts: Never, never, never speak without preparing first. Granted, there are some situations in life where you don't have a choice. There isn't much you can do about that. But always prepare if you have the opportunity. Write your key points on a note card, just in case. Your delivery will be more polished and you won't forget anything.

Don't make it about you. Even the hint that you are bragging about yourself will immediately nullify all the good you are doing by talking about the event and thanking others. Don't do it even if you do deserve all the credit. Your brothers and sisters know full well who did all the work. There is no need to rub their noses in it.

Finally, realize that as chapter president, you have been given a great learning opportunity. You get to practice speaking in front of others. This will help you with your career in the future.

How to Prepare for the Your Chapter Field Rep's Visit

> AS A NEW PRESIDENT, I WAS NOT PREPARED FOR OUR ANNUAL VISIT FROM OUR NATIONAL HEADQUARTERS. I DID NOT KNOW THE PURPOSE OF HIS VISIT, SO I WAS UNPREPARED FOR IT. I WAS ALSO SKEPTICAL THAT THE CONSULTANT WAS A SPY FROM NATIONALS JUST LOOKING TO GET US IN TROUBLE. IN HINDSIGHT, I WASTED A VERY VALUABLE OPPORTUNITY TO IMPROVE MY CHAPTER.

Nearly every fraternity or sorority will send a leadership consultant to visit your chapter once a year. The consultant is typically someone who graduated in the last year or two and travels the country advising chapters on behalf of the national organization.

The consultant is there to provide advice on how to improve your chapter. Of course, part of her role is to report her findings to the executive director. But she definitely isn't there to spy. She is there to help.

To prepare for the visit, you must talk to her well in advance of her arrival date. Here are some questions you should ask:

- Whom does she need to visit? The consultant likely will ask to visit the school's Greek adviser, your chapter adviser, and your chapter officers. You need to schedule these visits.
- What accommodations will the consultant need? Chances are, the chapter will be expected to put the consultant up. This means making sure he or she has a clean bed, not a couch in the corner. It also means making sure he or she has access to the Internet and a work space.
- Does the consultant want to address the chapter? She may or may not. Regardless, it is probably a good idea to have a chapter meeting coincide with the consultant's visit.
- Ask the consultant if there are any local attractions she wants to see. There is a good chance this will be the first time she has visited your school. You get to play tour guide and show off your great college or university. Be a good host or hostess.

These basic questions should put you in good shape for the visit. Here are a few things to remember:

- Don't break any rules, period. But especially while the consultant is on campus. The consultant is a brother. He's not looking to get the chapter into trouble. If you flaunt flagrant violations in his face, you are putting him in a bad spot. This isn't cool and definitely not how you should treat a fellow brother.
- Be sure your chapter knows the consultant is coming. If there are any members who want to talk to him, be sure to arrange that. It is especially important to get the new

members and younger members involved. They have a lot to gain from meeting a consultant.

- Don't forget that the consultant is a sister, and should be given the courtesy you would give any visiting sister. Invite her to meals and to hang out. Your consultant isn't paid much. She definitely didn't take the job for the money. She believes in what your sorority stands for and is eager to meet and connect with your chapter. Meet her half way.

- Put the consultant to work. If your chapter has issues that need to be resolved, get her assistance to help resolve them. Find out if she has any special skills or expertise. If she does, use them.

- Be sure to follow up with the consultant after the visit. If you played your cards right, you now have another great resource at your disposal. Be sure that you both hold each other accountable for whatever action items came out of the visit.

Follow these tips and instead of dreading the consultant's visit, you will actually look forward to it.

What is My Post-President Role?

I AM ABOUT TO END MY TERM AS PRESIDENT, AND IT'S BEEN A GREAT EXPERIENCE. HOWEVER, I STILL HAVE A YEAR LEFT IN SCHOOL AND I WANT TO REMAIN INVOLVED. BUT I DON'T WANT TO BE THAT KNOW-IT-ALL GUY IN THE CORNER OF THE CHAPTER MEETING WHO CAN'T LET THINGS GO. CAN YOU ADVISE ON WHAT ROLE A PRESIDENT SHOULD HAVE AFTER HIS TERM?

In my experience, there are two extremes in this situation. Some former presidents completely disappear after their terms. They are exhausted from the experience and relieved that it is over. Other presidents can't let go and undermine everything the new leadership team tries to do. Both of these extremes hurt the chapter.

Because of his or her experience, a former president is a very valuable resource for the chapter. He or she now serves a very important role as a mentor. Also, because the former president has been there, he or she knows the struggles that come with the job. There is nothing worse than someone who tries to undermine the new president's initiatives. Don't be that person.

In an ideal situation, when the president's term is over, she remains active and involved. However, the ex-president should not take on a leadership role. She's had her opportunity, and it is time for the younger members to lead.

The former president should start this new role during the transition meeting with her successor. She must make it clear to the new president that she is there to support her in any way she can. She will be a trusted confidante if advice is needed, and would be willing to help with any special initiatives the new president has.

Think about it from your perspective. How awesome would it have been if a former president came up to you and told you that she was there to support you in any way possible? Knowing that you have an ally in your corner is huge. You may not have had this advantage, but you can give it to the next president.

Transitioning from the front seat to any seat is tough for any Greek leader. It is almost a letdown in some ways. You may feel as though there is almost nothing left to accomplish.

Realize, though, that you will always be a leader to your chapter even if you don't hold a position. The younger members will watch how you conduct yourself and emulate you. They will come to you for advice. They will listen when you speak.

As someone who has been out of school for a few years now, let me give you a final, critical piece of advice: Your college career is ending fast. It will be over before you know it. You have worked your tail off for the chapter and with luck, you have gained the satisfaction of a job well done. You have learned skills that separate you from your peers and will make you successful in life.

Enjoy your last year of college without the responsibilities of being president. You have earned the opportunity to live it up and enjoy the fruits of your labor. Treat this as a victory lap and take it with grace and class. Focus on making memories and friendships, and take those into the real world with you. Someday you'll look back and these memories and friendships will bring a smile to your face. You'll realize that these are the most important parts of Greek life.

LEADERSHIP CHALLENGES

How to Deal with Criticism

> THE TOUGHEST PART OF BEING CHAPTER PRESIDENT WAS DEALING WITH THE CRITICISM FROM THE GENERAL MEMBERSHIP. I ALWAYS FELT THAT THE CHAPTER WAS GOSSIPING BEHIND MY BACK AND IT MADE BEING PRESIDENT VERY UNREWARDING. A PRESIDENT NEEDS TO HAVE THICK SKIN.

Criticism is healthy. It shows that the chapter isn't apathetic; it shows that members care. Aristotle said, "Criticism is something you can easily avoid by saying nothing, doing nothing, and being nothing."

As the president of your chapter, you obviously aspire to be the very best you can be. You aspire to take your chapter to new heights. You cannot do that unless you push your members outside their comfort zones. When you push them there, it is normal for them to feel a bit uneasy.

To ensure you are properly handling healthy criticism, you can do a few things. If you become aware that a member has issues with what the chapter is doing, confront her privately about it. Don't do so in a confrontational manner. Do so as someone who is looking for advice and seeking a respected opinion. Maybe her insight will help you improve what the chapter is doing. Don't be so stubborn as to believe your ideas can't be improved upon.

You have to remain above gossiping. If the president gossips; it will become infectious in the chapter. Take the high road and be above it. That is what leaders do.

Be sure to understand the reason behind the criticism. This can be a useful leadership tool for a president. Does the membership have valid concerns? Can they be used as a reason to plan a retreat? Does the chapter need to reevaluate its priorities? There is a chance you can gain useful insight from complaints and use it to improve the morale in your chapter.

Note that if you are unsure if the complaints are valid, ask another member you trust for her opinion. Sometimes you are too close to judge. Asking for someone else's opinion cannot hurt.

Finally, you must understand that criticism isn't personal. Every leader who has ever lived has been criticized. It comes with the position. Accept it with dignity and do your very best to lead the very best way you can. This is all you can do, and all that is expected of you.

CUTTING THE DEADWEIGHT

> MY CHAPTER HAS A NUMBER OF MEMBERS WHO ARE DEADWEIGHT TO THE CHAPTER. SOME DON'T PAY DUES AND RARELY COME AROUND. OTHERS ARE VERY BELLIGERENT AND DESTRUCTIVE WHEN THEY DO COME AROUND AND REFLECT POORLY ON THE CHAPTER. WHAT IS THE PROPER WAY TO EXPEL A MEMBER SO THE DAMAGE IS MINIMIZED?

I know there are deadbeats in your chapter because there are deadbeats in every chapter. The question is how you deal with them. Before you get to the point where you want to kick members out, make sure that this is the right course of action.

My chapter had a member who *never* came around. He was an older member who hadn't come around much since he was initiated. He was a good guy, but for whatever reason the fraternity never seemed to be a priority to him. He faithfully paid his dues every semester and then would disappear.

Some brothers wanted to kick this guy out. He wasn't bringing much to the table beyond paying his dues. A small group of us took a different approach, though: We went out of our way to invite him to participate. We'd invite him to lunch. We'd invite him to hang out. We'd invite him to fraternity functions even though no brother should ever need an invitation.

As our relationship grew, we asked why he didn't come around more. His response was that he'd had a lot going on in his personal life for the better part of two semesters. He felt that he had missed a lot by not being around much, and he lost touch with the brotherhood. As a result, he wasn't motivated to be a part of a fraternity of guys whom he didn't really know well anymore.

This changed when we reached out to rebuild the relationship. Before long, he started coming around more often and became a participating brother. It would have been a real shame if we'd lost this guy because we did not make the effort to keep him around.

So before you decide to kick someone out, you need to do two things. First, you need to make sure that it is the right decision. Are the member's actions really worth expulsion? Second, you need to make sure you know that member's side of the story. You do that by being a good sister or brother and having one-on-one conversations with the member in question.

During these one-on-one conversations, you will often find that the member who is up for expulsion will quit on his or her own if that is the right course of action. Most of the time, he or she is looking for a way out but avoids the conversation because he or she does not want to be seen as a quitter. It is easier to ignore it and hope it goes away. If you give this person the opportunity, he or she will probably jump at the chance to quit.

If you need to go through a formal expulsion process, then you need to follow your national headquarters' guidelines for expelling a member. Only the national headquarters has the ability to revoke membership. The local chapter does not have that authority.

Send an e-mail to your leadership consultant and ask for the process. Do not deviate from the instructions you receive.

Typically, the process starts with the local chapter making a recommendation to expel a member. The recommendation must be made in the form spelled out in your local bylaws.

This process needs to be well-thought-out because it is one of the most delicate situations you will face as president. Not only are you dealing with the feelings of the person who is being kicked out, but you are also dealing with members who probably feel strongly that the person in question should or should not be expelled.

I think the following steps are the best method for a chapter to determine whether to recommend expulsion.

1) A written request to expel a member is made to the executive committee. In this request, all reasons for expulsion need to be listed.
2) The executive board votes on whether to bring this request to a chapter vote. A simple majority of the executive board will determine if the measure passes. It is imperative that the executive board (led by the president) does not accept poor reasons for expulsion. For example, saying that the member isn't liked is not reason enough to expel. However, saying she is $1,000 behind in dues is. This should be a very private process.

3) If is the board decides that an expulsion vote is warranted, announce at the chapter meeting that a vote will take place during the next meeting on whether to expel the member in question. Distribute copies of the written request to each member. This week gives the members and the member in question enough time to do their homework so they make an informed vote.

4) At the next meeting, distribute the request again, and give the member in question an opportunity to respond. It is not a good idea to allow anyone else the opportunity to speak. Everyone should have had her opportunity to speak during the week between meetings. Nothing positive can come from opening the floor to the membership. After the member in question speaks, take a closed vote.

5) If the chapter votes to expel, follow your national headquarters' process for expulsion. If it doesn't, then you need to do some serious damage control to bring this member back into the fold.

If the member does escape the expulsion vote, the reprieve will be temporary. She will either quit or slowly drift away, which will lead to another expulsion hearing.

The most important thing at this point is to move on as quickly as possible. Be sure the chapter is confident in the decision and move forward. There is no need to dwell on the issue and let the bad taste linger in everyone's mouth. It stinks to kick someone out, and the quicker you can move on from the problem, the better off everyone will be.

CONFLICTS WITH OTHER CHAPTERS OR ORGANIZATIONS

OUR CHAPTER IS CONSTANTLY IN BATTLES WITH OTHER CHAPTERS ON OUR CAMPUS. EITHER WE ARE PICKING FIGHTS WITH THEM, OR THEY ARE PICKING FIGHTS WITH US. WHAT CAN I DO TO MAKE SURE OUR MEMBERS REALIZE THAT THIS TYPE OF THING DOES NOT HELP US?

It is easy to lump most of this under "guys being guys." There is nothing wrong with pranks, unless they are taken too far. As president, however, you need to realize that skirmishes and pranks can be counterproductive to what you are trying to accomplish.

In my experience, there are two main reasons Greeks partake in this type of mischief. The first reason is that members have nothing better to do. Boredom will force people to be creative when finding ways to spend their time.

A huge issue here is that most of this mischief goes way beyond the prank level and is illegal. Stealing things from the rival fraternity's chapter house is theft. "Painting" items on the rival fraternity's property is vandalism. As a leader, you cannot condone chapter participation in illegal activities.

Obviously, a healthy chapter will have fewer of these issues than a bored chapter has. Make sure the brothers have enough to worry about within their own chapter and they will leave other chapters alone.

The second condition in which mischief takes place is when there is friction between chapters because of boy/girl issues. This obviously affects both fraternities and sororities.

In theory, members' personal lives should not have an impact on the well-being of an organization. However, in a Greek chapter, your members' personal lives ARE the chapter.

The only way a president can combat this is to have a private conversation with the member who is at the head of the situation. You need to persuade him to be the bigger person and not let personal issues drive negative behavior in the chapter. You must stop the instigator in order to quash the problem. Realize that the friction won't be resolved until the instigator stops making trouble.

Of course, this doesn't really help if the other chapter is instigating the problem. If that is the case, you need to have a talk with the president of the other chapter. Let him know you realize that he cannot control every action of every person in his chapter, but you think both chapters would be better off without this type of animosity. With luck, he will agree and help you to diffuse the issue.

It may not be a bad idea to have an activity that will bring the two chapters together. This could be a great way for the chapters to get to know each other better and become allies instead of adversaries. If you can make the members become friends, then often the competition will turn into mutual respect.

Regardless of the issue, identify the ringleader early and persuade him to stop what he is doing. Focus his attention and efforts on more positive endeavors that will benefit both the chapter and the membership. This is the only way to end this type of problem.

Handling Probation

My challenges as chapter president have been unique in that I was elected as a sophomore. During my semester as a new member, our chapter was charged with alcohol and hazing infractions. As a result, we were suspended from campus for the better part of a year.

The university placed strict sanctions on our chapter in terms of hosting parties, philanthropic events, and new-member education sessions. The university asked the executive board to resign. All did. When elections were held the following fall, a fellow member of my pledge class and I were the only ones nominated for president.

I WON THE ELECTION. SINCE THEN, I HAVE FACED NUMEROUS CHALLENGES RELATED TO BEING PRESIDENT; MANY OF THEM RELATE TO OUR UNIQUE SITUATION AS A CHAPTER AND MY INEXPERIENCE AS A SOPHOMORE.

HOW DOES A CHAPTER IMPROVE AFTER HITTING ROCK BOTTOM WHILE ON PROBATION?

It is tough luck to find yourself on probation during your term as chapter president. Whatever dumb thing your chapter did to get you in trouble probably came on the previous person's watch. It is an unfortunate situation, but it is your responsibility to your chapter to make the very best of it.

In a way, this is a blessing to you as the president. You will have the opportunity to grow as a leader because of the trying times your chapter is experiencing. Think about it; it is easy to lead when the times are good. Anyone can lead during those times. But if you can successfully lead when the times are bad, then you will have gained skills that will help you to be successful for the rest of your life.

Your first step is to meet with the person who actually punished the chapter. In most cases, that would be the director of the Greek life office, the office of student conduct, the IFC, or the Panhellenic Council. You need to meet with him to understand fully the terms of your probation. You must introduce yourself to him and make sure he knows that abiding by his terms is a priority to you.

Whatever the terms are, it is imperative that your chapter abide by them. Getting in trouble while on probation is the type of thing that can get your chapter shut down. You definitely don't want that to happen on your watch.

Probation does not have to be a death sentence, though!

The most typical element of probation is eliminating the chapter's social events. While this stinks, it isn't the end of the world. You still have plenty of opportunities to party other places. You are most likely free to do everything else.

As president, your most critical leadership challenge will be to keep the morale of the members up during the probation period. Many members will think the world is ending because the chapter can't have parties. This simply isn't the case.

The best way to keep morale up is by making sure the members have something to look forward to. Everyone needs something to be excited about, and this will shift the focus away from the disappointment of being on probation.

Plan activities that aren't restricted by the terms of your probation.

- Take a road trip to another chapter.
- Take a road trip to another city.
- Go camping.
- Go whitewater rafting.
- Go to Vegas/Atlantic City.
- Go to a huge ball game.
- Focus on philanthropy.
- Play paintball.
- Go clay shooting.
- Go hunting.
- Have a huge cookout.
- Have huge tailgates.

- Host sports tournaments (alumni vs. undergrads, chapter vs. chapter, new members vs. actives — the possibilities are endless).
- Have dinner-date functions.
- Visit your national HQ.
- Attend a leadership seminar.
- Focus on new-member development.
- Invite the chancellor to speak to the chapter.
- Invite the football/basketball coach to speak to the chapter.

I came up with that list in about three minutes. You get the idea. The good thing about being on probation is that you have a lot of money in the social budget that can be spent elsewhere. Be creative and have fun with it.

Of course, be sure to plan a post-probation party for when your probation is completed. You know all the members will look forward to that.

Whatever you do, however, be sure to abide by the terms of the probation. If you are unsure, ask the person who put you on probation. Do not leave anything to chance.

Finally, use this as a learning opportunity. Your chapter had a serious breakdown if you ended up on probation. As president, it is your responsibility to identify this breakdown in your processes and fix it. Your chapter needs to learn from the mistakes it made and come out of probation stronger than ever. If you can do that, you will leave your chapter and successor in great shape.

Hazing

Hazing, the most frequently discussed aspect of Greek life, is still very prevalent. I think hazing still takes place because the conversation we have is usually about legality. But most eighteen- to twenty-two-year-olds don't understand the legal repercussions of their actions. Hazing also kills teamwork. You cannot build an effective organization with hazing because it breeds hate, mistrust, and fear. A good fraternity or sorority must work together, and hazing destroys this before it can even begin.

For your sake, I hope your chapter is a no-hazing chapter. If it isn't, you have your work cut out for you.

First, you need to know the facts:

Hazing isn't only a fraternity problem. In fact, studies show that hazing is more common in women's groups than in men's groups. This problem affects all Greeks.

Hazing is a crime. If someone is hurt, it becomes a felony. As president of your chapter, you will personally be held responsible to some extent, regardless of whether you were directly involved. If you are convicted of felony hazing, you will go to jail. Each state's law is different, as is every hazing case. Let's look at the recent Northern Illinois University hazing incident. A fraternity held an event in late 2012 at which a new member died of alcohol poisoning. (He had a 0.40 blood alcohol content.) Twenty-two brothers of the fraternity have been charged with hazing. Five have been charged with felony hazing. The five are the president, the vice president, the secretary, the new-member educator, and the brother who organized the event. Those five guys face from one to three years in prison if convicted.

This shows that if you are a leader of your chapter, you are responsible for what happens in your chapter. Realize that criminal charges are not the only possible repercussion. You undoubtedly will be kicked out of school. You will also probably face a civil lawsuit in which the harmed party or his family can collect money for the pain and suffering caused.

If you are involved in a felony crime, your chance of leading a good life is slim. It will be nearly impossible to get back into a good school or be hired for a good job.

And let's not forget for a second the victims of hazing. It is unconscionable to treat someone who is supposed to become one of your closest friends—a brother or sister—or anyone, for that matter, with callous disregard for his or her comfort or safety.

So for those obvious reasons, you absolutely cannot be involved in hazing or allow hazing to take place at your chapter.

However, the less obvious reasons are just as significant. Hazing turns your chapter into a fraud. During the new-member period, you are building the foundation for brotherhood or sisterhood. If you build this foundation on lies and deceit through hazing, you will create a cycle in which members distrust and resent each other.

But if you are reading this book, you probably realize all of this. Strong leaders understand the ill effects of hazing. Their problem is how to convince the rest of the membership that it is wrong.

Let's address this question by tackling the three common reasons some chapters continue to haze:

1. **"The pledge has to earn his membership."** I wholeheartedly agree with this one. Joining a Greek organization is an honor. Membership is exclusive. We should only allow the most qualified people into our organizations. However, they can prove their worthiness by means other than hazing.

2. **"You have to break pledges down to build them back up. This is what the military does, and it produces the best leaders in the world."** This is nonsense. I was an officer in the military, and that is not how it works. The military takes individuals who show potential (which is why it has such an extensive recruiting program) and makes them a better version of themselves. There is no hazing or breaking anyone down. If someone can't cut it, the military weeds him out. The military trains officers by giving them a number of tasks that they cannot possibly accomplish in the time allotted. This forces officers to be efficient—to be

smart in how they prioritize tasks. This instills discipline. It also instills confidence because officers learn that they can do more than they thought was possible. This is how the military teaches leadership, and they are the best in the world at it.

3. **"This is how I became a brother/sister, and I'm not going to stop a tradition."** This is tough one to counter because it isn't a very intellectual argument. If this mindset were prevalent everywhere in the world, then there would never be any improvement. I would deal with this reason by continually asking, "Why can't we be better?" If your chapter members don't want to improve, then you are talking to a lost cause.

Changing a chapter with a hazing culture into a nonhazing chapter is difficult. As the president, however, you have the obligation to do it to protect your new members from being hazed. You have the obligation to protect your members from themselves. You also have the obligation to keep the relationships your members have with each other healthy. Challenge your new members, but do so in a way that doesn't demean them. This is how you keep your chapter and Greek life strong.

How to Handle the Reaction to Gay Members

HOW DO YOU HANDLE GAY MEMBERS? WE HAVE HAD SITUATIONS WHERE A GAY BROTHER BRINGS HIS DATE TO A FRATERNITY FUNCTION, WHICH UPSETS SOME OF OUR ALUMNI. WE HAVE HAD SITUATIONS WHERE BROTHERS STARTED DATING. THIS HAS CAUSED A LOT OF FRICTION IN OUR CHAPTER. HOW DOES A PRESIDENT ADDRESS THIS?

Your main responsibility as the president of your chapter is to lead, even when leading isn't easy.

It is never easy to confront angry alumni/alumnae. You owe them respect for all they have done for the chapter. However, this does not mean appeasing them if their views are shortsighted and are not in accordance with the values of your fraternity or sorority.

Engaging an alumnus or alumna in a values-based discussion is the proper way to address this issue. Explain that the member in question exemplifies the values and characteristics that are at the heart of the fraternity or sorority's mission. The member's sexual orientation is irrelevant to his or her standing as a member.

If the alum is still angry, you have a choice. You can either turn your back on your brother or sister to appease the alum, or you can stand up for what is right. What is right in this situation is backing your brother or sister.

Handling members who are dating is an entirely different issue. This situation can tear a chapter apart. Your chapter is a place to build brotherhood or sisterhood while you strive to become better men and women. This cannot be accomplished with the distraction of members dating.

As president, you need to do everything in your power to make sure the chapter understands that this type of relationship between members isn't tolerated. Realize that this does not mean passing judgment on the relationship. It means that it is unhealthy for members to date because of the issues that will certainly occur. What happens when they break up? Can they go back to being just brothers or sisters? What about room assignments? Do you want dating members shacking up at the house? What happens during lovers' quarrels? Do you want your membership to be involved on both sides of that drama?

To be honest, if it has gotten to this stage, it is almost too late. You will have a major problem on your hands that will most likely involve one or both members leaving the chapter.

Unfortunately, there is no "one size fits all" solution to this problem. Whatever action you take, be sure to keep the longevity of the chapter in mind. Do what needs to be done and move on. Focus on the positive and the future of the chapter. It will guide you to make the right decision.

How to Deal with a Member Who Wants to Quit

THIS ISSUE CAME UP A COUPLE TIMES WHEN I WAS PRESIDENT OF MY CHAPTER. A MEMBER WOULD KNOCK ON MY DOOR OUT OF THE BLUE AND SAY THAT HE WANTED TO QUIT. SOMETIMES A NEW MEMBER WANTED TO QUIT; SOMETIMES IT WAS AN INITIATED MEMBER. A PRESIDENT NEEDS TO BE PREPARED TO HANDLE THIS SITUATION.

When an initiated member decides to quit, she isn't just telling you that she no longer wants to be a part of the chapter. She is telling you that she doesn't want to be your friend anymore. Furthermore, she is telling you that the chapter isn't worth her time or money, and that she is OK with losing the friends she has made.

If this happens, it should come as a pretty big blow to the president. This essentially means that the chapter has failed this member, and that chapter leadership let it happen.

Unfortunately, it probably isn't worth your time to try to convince her to stay. You don't need members who are not fully committed to the chapter. It is better for everyone to cut her losses and move on.

I had this very conversation with brothers in my chapter and convinced a lot of them to stay. But the reprieve was only temporary, as their hearts were no longer in the chapter. They all quit eventually.

While this situation is unfortunate, it can become a valuable lesson for a president. You need to find out the true reason why a member wants to quit. Finding out will be hard. The member who is quitting will not want to tell you. He will say that he doesn't have the time or the money, or that his heart is no longer in it. If you let him get away with giving you these types of answers, you are doing your chapter a disservice.

You need to dig deeper to find out more. There is a problem lurking somewhere, or the member would not be quitting. You need to explain to the quitting member that he can share these issues with you in confidence. Explain to him that you cannot fix the problem he has for the rest of the chapter unless you know what it is. With luck, you will be able to find out what it is, and you can use this information to improve your chapter.

The story is different if a new member tries to quit. More than likely, this is an indictment on your new-member period. If you haze or if your chapter is too demanding, initiates will be turned off.

It is stupid to lose a potential lifelong brother or sister because the demands of the new-member period are too overwhelming. It is very difficult to find high-quality new members. Don't lose them for dumb reasons.

I am not saying you need to lower your standards to make sure all new members make it through your new-member period. That would be foolish. What I am saying is that you need to make sure your new-member program isn't a barrier for getting quality men or women initiated into your chapter.

Finally, just as with initiated members, you need to realize why the new member feels the way he does and use this information to improve your chapter. People could be quitting for something completely unrelated to the new-member period. Maybe they are having personal problems that you don't know about.

Talking to members who are contemplating quitting will always be tough. Attrition is just part of the life of a chapter. Don't be afraid to lose people who aren't fully committed. But don't let them go without finding out why. This could be valuable information that will improve your chapter over the long run.

How to Handle Online Flame-Wars

A HUGE CHALLENGE TO CHAPTER PRESIDENTS IS ADDRESSING E-MAIL LISTSERV OR FACEBOOK FLAME WARS. IT'S DIFFICULT ENOUGH TO MODERATE A HEATED MEETING, BUT TRY PUTTING OUT A FIRE THAT'S TAKING PLACE ON AN ONLINE MEDIUM. IT IS EXTREMELY DIFFICULT.

This can be a difficult situation. There is no shortage of Internet tough guys out there. In real life, they are pansies, but armed with a smart phone, they think they are badass.

If this happens in your chapter, there is only one way you can put an end to it. That is by speaking to the offending parties in person and convincing them to stop what they are doing.

You need to explain to them that it hurts the chapter when they air their dirty laundry online. Explain that it makes them look small and petty. Explain to them that it would be much better if they talked the issue out in person.

They will do one of two things. They will agree and stop, or they will keep flaming. If it is a purely personal issue, let them flame away. Sure, they will look dumb, but that is their problem. You tried to help. It will probably provide cheap entertainment. As president of the chapter, though, you need to stay out of it since it is not a chapter issue.

If it *is* a chapter issue, however, it is a different story. If the offenders won't listen to you, enlist a few other members to try to intercede on the chapter's behalf. The chapter's dirty laundry should never be aired in public. It makes everyone look bad and will have a lasting effect on outsiders who are witnesses to this pathetic display.

Be sure to bring the issue up at the next chapter meeting. The entire chapter needs to hear the message from the president that this type of behavior is not appreciated or condoned.

It is a sad reality that small, negative events can sully the campus opinion of a chapter. They quickly wash away months of positive contributions to the community and the university. Do not let chapter disagreements become public. No one wins when you air your dirty laundry. A strong chapter can weather disagreements between members and keep the discourse out of the public eye.

How to Handle Seniors Who Don't Come Around Anymore

> As I entered the second half of my junior year in college and the second year of my status as a member, I find myself less enamored by the chapter. This whole idea of senioritis has plagued my chapter for quite some time and I think it would be worthwhile to know some techniques of getting older members involved with younger members.

There is nothing sadder than seeing a member who led the chapter as a sophomore and junior disappear as senior. Put yourself in his shoes for a minute, though.

Attrition is natural. There will always be more young members than there are older members. Probably only half of a senior's new-member class is still around. They quit, flunk out, graduate early, transfer, etc.

Seniors' interests and priorities have changed. They are now focusing on graduation and getting a job. They are probably in a steady relationship, and the last thing their significant other wants to do is to chill at the house.

When seniors don't have an influential role in the planning of chapter events, the chapter tends to hold events that cater to the younger members. This further dissuades the older member from coming around. And when older members do come around, they usually catch a ration of grief from younger members who have contributed a tenth of what the older member has in his time in the chapter.

It is pretty easy to see why older members stay away. But if your chapter sounds like what I just described, then shame on you. As the president of your chapter, it is your job to make sure all members feel they are getting value from their membership. That means you need to have events that keep both the younger members and older members happy.

Fortunately, the older members aren't difficult to please. They don't want much, and if they stuck around until senior year, they obviously feel a deep connection to the chapter. Make it a point to toss them a bone every once in a while by having events that they would like. Obvious ideas of events that older members would want to attend are tailgate parties at football games and semiformal and formal date functions. Many older members like stay active in athletics, so be sure there is room for them on the intramural teams.

The biggest thing you can do is to make sure they feel appreciated when they do come to the house. If they feel welcome, and they know that the members are genuinely glad to see them, then chances are they will make it a point to come around more often.

You can also use these older members as mentors. Go to lunch with them and pick their brains on how to improve the chapter. Ask them what they are going through with trying to graduate and get a job, and ask for advice on how you can be better prepared when you get there.

Your goal as a leader needs is to make sure every member feels wanted and appreciated. And you are failing if you don't make the oldest members feel respected and needed.

Inactive Status

A PRESIDENT SHOULD BE PREPARED TO
DEAL WITH MEMBERS WHO WANT TO GO
"INACTIVE." THESE MEMBERS COULD HAVE
FINANCIAL ISSUES OR LIFE ISSUES. SOME MAY
WANT TO TAKE A SEMESTER OFF AND COME
BACK. REGARDLESS, THIS COULD OPEN THE
DOOR TO BIG PROBLEMS.

I despise the thought of an inactive status. When you were initiated, you agreed to become a member for life, not for when it is convenient. You made that commitment when you went through your ritual.

There is no doubt being a member is sometimes tough. Maybe money is tight or the demands of your academic program leave you with little time to devote to the chapter. Part of what makes Greek life special is that we all have those times, and we can help each other through them. This is a huge part of growth and learning. If a member thinks he is better off not being part of the chapter, then he is missing that point.

My chapter wrestled with this notion when I was an undergraduate brother and actually created an inactive status. Several members took advantage of it. Here is what happened: They became inactive but still participated in chapter functions like full members. The only things they skipped were the chapter meetings. Active members started to resent the inactive members because they had all the benefits of being a full member but did not have the same financial commitment. Eventually, we stopped having an inactive status, and *every single inactive member quit.*

One thing you need to realize is that your national headquarters does not recognize an inactive status. This means that you will still be required to pay the national dues for members who go inactive. This will put an unfair financial burden on your chapter.

If this issue comes up during your term as president, be sure you stop the conversation immediately. Remind your members that either you are a member of the chapter or you aren't. If you don't want to be a member, then turn in your badge. There is no gray area in brotherhood or sisterhood.

Peter Pan Alums

One issue that may take all the tact and diplomacy skills a president can muster is the Peter Pan alum. I've come across two forms of them: the ones who just won't grow up and want to relive their chapter experiences all over again, and the ones who want the chapter to stay the way it was when they were involved and will do anything to keep it that way. Either type can be detrimental to chapter morale and cohesion.

There is nothing worse than someone who just can't let it go — especially if he is a respected alumnus of the chapter. This type of member can cause all sorts of problems. He comes to the house once in a blue moon. When he visits, he inevitably parties too hard and then takes it out on the new members.

The aftermath is worse, though. The members of your chapter are impressionable. They will think his behavior is cool and that they should act that way. The membership will use this alumni's example to justify their poor behavior in the future.

In short, this alumnus can undermine the hard work of several generations of chapter leaders. As a result, it is imperative that you have a plan in place to handle this situation. The goal of your plan must be to remove the offending alumnus from the situation where he will cause damage.

This plan must be formulated during a five-minute talk you have with your executive board early in your term—*before* you have an issue. If you wait to develop your plan until the problem happens, it is too late. You will have a difficult time getting support from your leadership team, and disaster will ensue.

When this ugly situation occurs, diffuse it by being creative. Have a few members pull the Peter Pan alum aside for a mentoring session. That is, the current members ask the alum to mentor them. Feed his ego and occupy his time by getting his thoughts on what the chapter needs to do to improve. Ask his about his glory days and get him to tell those stories.

While the alum is being distracted, be sure that someone on your leadership team tells the new members to go home. You don't want them around this situation. They can only be a target for trouble.

This plan will eliminate your two biggest concerns—an ugly confrontation with an alum and new-member hazing.

Within a few days of Peter Pan's visit, the president must call him and thank him for the insight he provided during the mentoring session. Let him know that the membership got a ton of information and ideas from his mentorship, and you appreciate it.

Also, ask the alum to tone down any negative behavior he exhibits. Let him know that you want the chapter to party like it's 1999 too, but as a distinguished alumnus of the chapter, he must provide an example for the younger members.

Admittedly, this conversation is difficult for a chapter president to have. However, the president has to do this for the good and welfare of the chapter.

If the offending alum insists on continuing his bad behavior after this talk, then the membership needs to let him know that his actions do not fit with the values of the chapter, and he is no longer welcome unless he changes his behavior.

One of the major responsibilities of a chapter president is to ensure the longevity of the chapter. If the president allows negative influences to infiltrate the chapter, it won't take long for negative behaviors to snowball among the members. Eliminate minor problems before they become major ones.

Who Should Live in the House?

> WE'VE HAD ISSUES WITH MEMBERS FEELING ENTITLED TO LIVE IN THE HOUSE, WHEN IN REALITY, THERE ARE OTHER MEMBERS WHO ARE BETTER FOR THE ORGANIZATION. I'VE HAD A HECK OF A TIME GETTING AROUND "RITUAL ORDER" AND FOCUSING ON WHAT'S BEST FOR THE CHAPTER. A PRESIDENT MUST BE PREPARED TO HANDLE THESE DIFFICULT SITUATIONS FOR THE BETTERMENT OF THE CHAPTER.

I recently spoke to a brother from another fraternity at my school who was complaining about his new house. One of chapter's wealthy alums donated money to build a mansion that slept forty guys. However, the chapter could not fill a house that big and eventually lost it. So, on the surface, your problem looks like a great problem to have. It definitely is better than losing the house.

While I see your point on wanting the best group of members possible to live in the house, you can't fight this battle as chapter president. As president, you are not the chapter's ultimate authority; you are its top arbitrator. You are charged with treating each brother fairly and equally. You can't possibly fulfill that responsibility if you are picking favorites to live in the house.

My advice is to abide by the predetermined pecking order. It makes sense to me that priority would go to those who lived in the house last year, and vacancies would be filled by seniority. Regardless of how your chapter allocates rooms, document the process.

If your chapter has this problem, I would do two things. First, I would raise the rent. If rooms in the house are in high demand, the chapter should be compensated for it.

Second, I would try to accommodate as many members living in the house as possible. My chapter did this by renovating a laundry room and turning it into a bedroom. This cost us a couple thousand bucks up front, but enabled us to get another member in the house at $600 a month. This was a great investment for our chapter. Also, encourage members to double up in rooms if they aren't already doing so.

These two things can have a dramatic impact on the finances of the chapter. As president, you have the duty to maximize the value of one of your most important assets—the house.

That said, there are certain instances when you can attempt to manipulate who lives in the house. If there is a member with drug issues, then it is best to remove him from the house. If there is a member who is no longer a student, then he should not get preference over a member who is taking classes. If there is a member who is not in good financial standing with the chapter, he should lose his priority for living in the house. If there is a member who cannot commit to living in the house for an entire year, then he should lose his spot to a member who can.

It's important to note that none of these instances involves giving one member preference over another for personal reasons. As president you can never show favoritism—especially when it comes to something as important as a member's living arrangements.

PREVENTING AND HANDLING CRISES

COPING WITH CRISES AT THE HOUSE

An expected scenario I encountered as chapter president was dealing with the media after a risk-management incident happened at the house. Our chapter handled it badly, and it reflected very poorly on us. Every president should know how to respond to a risk-management crisis.

The very first thing to do during a crisis is to make sure the incident is contained. This means making sure all members are safe. If a member is seriously injured and does not have the ability to alert his family, then you need to do this for him. This also means making sure the chapter is no longer in danger of the negative impact of whatever occurred.

Then you can start damage control. First, make sure that all members know that the president is the only one allowed to speak to outsiders about the incident. If anyone is asked a question, he must refer it to the president to answer. It sounds obvious, but it is important that the membership understands that the president is not on a power trip. Rather, the president is responsible for gathering all the facts and getting advice from trusted alumni based on those facts. This will ensure the story released to the public is accurate and does not conflict with any other report.

Next, the president must gather all the facts. This is crucial to maximize the value of the following step, which is seeking counsel from a trusted adviser.

To get the facts, the president needs to talk to those directly involved in the incident. He also must talk to any witnesses. Be sure to get contact info from those you don't know in case you need to talk to them further. Having a clear understanding of what happened and who was involved is essential for getting good advice from a trusted adviser. If an outsider tries to speak to the president before he gets counsel, he must politely say, "We are still gathering facts and are not prepared to make a statement at this time."

The trusted adviser should be the chapter adviser. If he isn't available, then the Greek life director, a faculty adviser, or someone from your headquarters staff will be able to help. The key is to seek advice from someone outside the undergraduate chapter who has experience and will have an unbiased view of the issue. This adviser will direct the president to the resources he needs to prepare for talking to the media and other outsiders. The adviser will put the president in contact with a lawyer from the national fraternity/sorority if necessary. They will help him to prepare a statement. This is one of the reasons why you belong to a national organization. The national headquarters has the ability and resources to support you during trying times. This connection is better than gold in your time of need.

The adviser will also be there to help with the next critical step, which is putting your chapter back together after the dust settles. There will be significant fallout after any crisis.

Finally, be sure to call an emergency chapter meeting as soon as possible to let the rest of the chapter know firsthand what is going on. You want to prevent the rumor mill from starting. Getting everything out in the open and everyone on the same page is essential to putting the crisis behind you.

Dealing with a crisis is something that no president ever envisions when he takes office. Realize that the potential is out there and that you need to be prepared.

Selling Prescription Drugs at the Chapter House

Our chapter had a big issue with brothers selling their prescription drugs out of the chapter house. This issue completely blindsided me as president. I'd like to know how we should handle brothers selling prescription drugs.

It is alarming how prevalent this activity has become. Drugs like Adderall are commonly abused as study aids. The abuse of prescription drugs is a terrible thing, but it's not nearly as bad as the sale of them. If a brother is selling his prescription drugs to others, he is a drug dealer in the eyes of the law. This means that if he is caught, he could go to jail for a very long time. This means, in turn, that if he is caught selling drugs at the chapter house, there is a very good chance that the chapter will lose its charter and be closed down. If other brothers are found to have assisted the brother who is dealing (in ways that can be as simple as giving a ride) then they may get into huge trouble too.

This is one of the greatest risk-management issues you can face as chapter president. If you become aware that members are dealing drugs, your responsibility is unequivocal. You must do everything possible to stop it. You owe it to the offending member, who probably is not aware of the consequences of his actions. As your brother's keeper, you need to protect him from himself and make sure he realizes what he is doing. In the perfect world, this conversation will convince him to stop.

If it doesn't, you must ratchet up the pressure. Enlist other brothers to convince him to stop. If that doesn't work, involve your chapter adviser. If that fails, get his parents involved. And if that doesn't work, you need to involve the university. More than likely, the university will involve the authorities.

Explain to the brother that this will be your course of action. Let him know that you hope it doesn't get to the last step, because that could mean he'd end up in jail. Of course, if it goes that far, the offending brother will probably end up hating you and the fraternity. You will feel like crap the entire time. Many brothers will look at you as the bad guy and not understand why you are singling out this brother.

Keep in mind that you did not cause this situation. There is a brother in your chapter dealing drugs. That is a felony. He is breaking the law, not you. You are doing the right thing. You need to have the courage and conviction to stand up for what is right. Also, realize that your actions could keep this brother out of jail. You are ensuring that he gets to enjoy his twenties and thirties instead of spending them locked up.

You also are making sure that drugs don't get in the hands of people who abuse them. Drug abuse is one of the surest ways to ruin a life. You are helping to prevent that from happening. Finally, you are upholding your responsibility to protect your chapter, your charter, and your brotherhood.

Leadership isn't always easy. If you encounter this situation, it will be especially trying. You owe it to your chapter, your brothers, and your community to do the right thing.

How to Deal with Drinking and Driving

FIGURING OUT HOW TO DEAL WITH MEMBERS
WHO WANT TO DRIVE HOME DRUNK HAS
BEEN A HUGE HEADACHE FOR ME AS CHAPTER
PRESIDENT. I WISH SOMEONE HAD GIVEN
ME MORE GUIDANCE ON HOW TO PERSUADE
MEMBERS OF MY CHAPTER THAT THIS IS A
BAD IDEA.

I had to bury a fraternity brother who was killed by a drunken driver. My brother, Dennis, was the first one on the scene of a car accident in the middle of an intersection. A drunken driver in a van sped through the intersection, killing six people, including Dennis. Dennis was twenty-four.

Seeing the hurt and pain of his friends and family was one of the most difficult things I have been through. No one should die that way or that young.

You know as well as I do that your brothers and sisters will drink. It is your job as a leader in your fraternity or sorority to establish a culture in which driving after drinking is seen as unacceptable behavior. That is a hard culture to create, but it is critically important that you do so. Let's face it, statistics show that the leading cause of death for people in their late teens and early twenties is auto accidents, and large percentage of those accidents are due to alcohol.

So how do you create the culture that driving drunk is unacceptable?

The first way is by being the example. Other members will emulate the chapter president. If the chapter president has no problem driving after she's had too many beers, then her sisters (especially the youngest ones) will think that this is acceptable behavior. The president always leads by example.

Another way to create the right culture is by having the courage to initiate difficult talks with members of your chapter who are displaying bad behavior. If a sister is in the act of going for her car after drinking too much, you should calmly offer a better solution. Realize that drunks are confrontational by nature, and you want to avoid an argument at all costs.

If the act has already been committed, it is natural to feel relieved that everyone made it home safely and then move on. But if you don't bring the issue up with the offending member, you are not fulfilling your role as leader. Again, do not make the conversation confrontational. Focus on your concern for her and your concern for others.

Another way to create the right culture is through education. No one in your chapter has been driving or drinking for very long. They do not have the experience or knowledge to understand when they have had too many drinks to get behind the wheel. Bring in someone from the university to do a short presentation on the effects of driving drunk at your next chapter meeting. A guy from our school brought a set of goggles that simulated being drunk. Then he had us walk a line to show the impact of alcohol consumption on motor skills. He also brought a chart that explained how many drinks would get us drunk. The low number of drinks it takes to be legally drunk was startling for the members of our chapter.

Another thing your chapter can do is buy a breathalyzer. You can find them on Amazon; they cost a couple hundred bucks. If you have one on hand, you will have no problem settling an argument with a member who says she is sober enough to drive.

Finally, the best way to create a culture in which driving drunk is unacceptable is to plan around it. For chapter functions, assign designated drivers. If you can't find people to do that, then hire a van and driver for the night. It will be the best couple of hundred bucks your chapter spends that night. When members go out, be sure there's a plan to get them home safely before they leave. Plans made when everyone has already been drinking are rarely good.

This is a difficult situation. No one wants to be the bad guy in the chapter. The risk of not doing so is too great, however. Your role as a leader is to protect your brothers or sisters from bad situations—even the ones they create for themselves.

Eating Disorders and Substance Abuse

My chapter has over eighty members. As a result, we have a wide range of personal issues that I was unprepared to deal with. Some of the most difficult were members with eating disorders and substance abuse problems. What can a president do to combat those problems?

According to a March 15, 2007, article in *USA Today*, 23 percent of college students meet the clinical definition of chemically dependent. According to a December 27, 2012, article in *USA Today*, 25 percent of students have eating disorders. Note that eating disorders are not just a women's problem — 10 percent to 15 percent of students with eating disorders are male.

In other words, this means that potentially a quarter of your chapter is abusing drugs/alcohol and a quarter has eating disorders. Those are alarming statistics. As president, this can seem to be a daunting leadership challenge. These are serious, real-life issues, and you may feel unprepared to address them.

Know that it is OK not to have all the answers. A president just can't solve some problems. However, the president does need to do three things with regard to eating disorders and substance abuse:

1. You need to be connected with every member enough to recognize signs of problems. It is easy to lose touch with your brothers and sisters when you are in a leadership role. An endless list of tasks and responsibilities require your attention. You cannot let this be an excuse for failing to recognizing a problem in one of your brothers or sisters. Being connected to your membership is only half that battle. The other half is recognizing the symptoms of abuse and eating disorders. Some of these symptoms are obvious; some are not. Be sure to spend a few minutes on the Internet learning what those symptoms are.

2. If you suspect a problem, you must have the courage to talk to the person about it. Many times, your gut will let you know there is a problem before you identify the classic symptoms. If you suspect there's an issue, put it on the table. Needless to say, this will be awkward and difficult. Remember, you are not a counselor. You are a concerned friend. You are there to let a member know that you care and to help her to get help.

3. You need to know where members can go for help. It is best to have a few different options so the person who needs help can feel in control of the decision. Your school employs professionals who are trained to handle these issues. They will have published literature. Be sure you have access to that information in case you need it.

These are very difficult issues. If you have a member who is suffering from these problems, you will have to handle it delicately. Your goal is not to solve the problem. The member will not stop doing the behavior that is hurting her until she wants to stop. Your goal is to get her the help she needs. This will require you to be a good friend by showing concern. You have to be persistent in case your initial attempts to help are rebuffed.

While this is hard, it could be the most important thing you do as a leader in your chapter. These types of problems can ruin lives. You can be the person responsible for helping someone turn around her life. There isn't much that is more rewarding than that.

ALCOHOL POISONING

HOW DOES A PRESIDENT HANDLE A SITUATION IN WHICH A MEMBER POTENTIALLY HAS ALCOHOL POISONING? IF IT HAPPENS AT A FUNCTION, IT COULD BE A HUGE BLACK EYE ON THE FRATERNITY OR SORORITY. HOW DO WE GET THE MEMBER THE HELP HE NEEDS WITHOUT GETTING THE CHAPTER IN TROUBLE?

When I was chapter president, the vice president drank way too much at a party at our house, and we found him passed out on the couch after the party.

No one knew how much he'd had to drink that night, but we knew it was a lot. He'd been glued to a half gallon of Jim Beam that entire night, and the bottle was nearly empty when we found him. We became scared when he would not wake up. We didn't know what to do.

Of course we wanted to make sure our brother was OK. But we didn't want to overreact to the point where we got him or the chapter in trouble. We had a decision to make. Do we call 911? Or do we toss him in bed and hope he sleeps it off?

Since the risk of alcohol poisoning was a far greater threat than the chapter or our brother potentially getting in trouble, we called 911. When the paramedics arrived, they revived him with smelling salts. They checked his vitals and said he was OK—he just needed to sleep it off.

The next day, I called our Greek life director and explained what had happened. I was unsure if we would be punished, but I wanted her to hear what had happened from me in order to minimize any potential damage. To my disbelief, we did not get in trouble for our actions that night; instead, we were commended for being responsible.

Of course, looking back I can see where we had several risk-management breakdowns. First, we did not have anyone who was sober at the time to evaluate the situation rationally. There needs to be at least one sober, responsible member of the organization present at each function. Second, no one stopped the vice president from binge drinking. We all saw what he was doing, but none of us took the time to stop him. Third, we had no idea how to tell if the brother had alcohol poisoning, and we had no clue what to do if he did.

According to the Mayo Clinic website, to tell if someone has alcohol poisoning, you need to look for these signs:

- Confusion, stupor
- Vomiting
- Seizures
- Slow breathing (less than eight breaths a minute)

- Irregular breathing (a gap of more than ten seconds between breaths)
- Blue-tinged skin or pale skin
- Low body temperature (hypothermia)
- Unconsciousness ("passing out"), the person can't be roused

If someone is showing these symptoms, call 800-222-1222 (in the United States), and your call will automatically be routed to your local poison control center. The staff at the poison control center or emergency call center can tell you whether you should call an ambulance, take the person directly to a hospital, or put him to bed. All calls to poison control centers are confidential.

I know chapters are afraid of getting in trouble, especially if underage drinking is involved. But fear of punishment is a horrible reason to put someone's life at risk. Being responsible is hard and sometimes not much fun. One last thing to remember is that you did not cause this situation; the offending brother or sister did. You are responding to a situation caused by his or her irresponsibility. As a result, you should not feel badly about doing the right thing.

How to Deal with Rape

A SISTER IN MY SORORITY ALLEGED SHE WAS RAPED. SHE HAD THE REPUTATION OF BEING PROMISCUOUS. AS A RESULT, SOME OF THE SISTERS BELIEVED HER, AND SOME DID NOT. THIS CAUSED A HUGE DIVIDE IN OUR CHAPTER THAT I WAS UNPREPARED FOR AS CHAPTER PRESIDENT.

Let me start by saying I am not the least bit qualified to give advice on this subject. Due to that fact, I thought about omitting the topic of rape from this book. However, sexual assault is too important a topic to leave out. If nothing else, I want you to be aware of the impact that sexual assault can have on your chapter and on your members.

The most common type of rape situation is dramatically different for sororities than it is for fraternities. Typically, a woman is the victim and a man is the perpetrator. If your chapter is involved in a sexual assault crime, it will have a profound impact on your membership. It is one of the most serious situations you can encounter, and it will test your leadership ability.

Here are my thoughts on how the president of each type of chapter should handle a sexual assault situation.

For sorority presidents: The majority of sexual assault situations in sororities entails a sister being victimized. If this happens in your chapter, you need to be prepared with the right answers so you can help your sister in need. Your university will have a sexual assault policy. Read it and make sure you understand it. Be sure you know where to go to get help, should the need arise.

Also, be sure your membership understands the importance of taking care of one another. If a sister is putting herself in a dangerous situation, another sister has to step up and remove her from it. It is essential that you take care of each other.

Should you find out that a sister has been raped, call 911 and get her to a hospital. Do not let her shower, as this will remove the evidence of the crime.

There is a chance that she will not want to report the rape. Most often, sexual assault occurs between people who know each other, and more than 95 percent of rapes go unreported. Maybe she was drinking underage and does not want that information to get out. Maybe she feels guilty because she put herself in a bad situation. Maybe she does not want to draw that type of attention to herself.

Regardless of her hesitation, as a leader, you must try to convince her to do the right thing and report the crime. If she doesn't, another girl might be raped in the future. Let her know that there are victims' rights, which include confidentiality. Again, you must understand the policy of your state and your school so you can provide the best advice possible.

Getting immediate attention for her is just the first step. This type of traumatic experience will have a lingering impact on the sisterhood. Be sure the sister has access to professional help. Be sure to be more active in supporting your sister as she deals with the aftermath of this horrific crime.

Finally, don't discount the impact the incident will have on the rest of the chapter. A sexual assault accusation can tear a chapter apart. Sexual assault is much bigger than the operations of a chapter. As such, the chapter should unequivocally support its sister until the proper authorities conclude their investigation.

As president, you must make sure that the sisterhood does not deviate from this message. If there are sisters who do not want to be supportive, inform them to keep their thoughts to themselves. Your membership will follow the lead of the president during crises. If you handle yourself in a professional manner, then the rest of the chapter will as well.

This is an extremely difficult situation for any sorority president to face. Be sure to lean on your advisers for help. Remember that sometimes the best leaders are the ones who show they care the most.

For fraternity presidents: If a sexual assault situation occurs in your chapter, it will most likely be that a brother has been accused. Even though someone from your chapter is not the victim, it is important to understand the university's sexual assault policy and to educate the membership on it.

As president, you need to take certain steps to ensure this does not happen in your chapter. You need to create a safe environment for women. This means developing a membership that takes pride in being gentlemen, and maintaining a house does not have any areas that would be deemed unsafe.

You must instill the attitude that all of your guests, especially women, will be protected from bad situations. Should a potentially bad situation present itself, a brother should take steps immediately to eliminate the problem. Often, this means taking care of guests who have had too much to drink. Getting these guests home safely is the responsibility of the chapter. It should not be taken lightly.

It also means stepping in when a situation doesn't seem right. If a brother or guest is making unwanted advances on a woman, then it must be stopped. The person who steps up and does the right thing should be supported. Standing by and doing nothing should not be viewed as acceptable behavior.

While that is easy to say, it is much more difficult to instill this mindset in a brotherhood. It starts with recruiting the right type of guy. It is essential to make being a gentleman an important part of the new-member program. It is also important that older members of the chapter lead by example.

If your chapter can do these three things, then it will be easier to create a culture that respects women.

If a sexual assault accusation is made, you must take some critical steps, especially if the assault is alleged to have happened at the chapter house.

First, you need to call your chapter adviser and your national headquarters and inform them of the situation. You need to do this immediately; it cannot wait. They will provide the immediate support and guidance that you will need.

Second, you need to create a clear separation between the sexual assault situation and the chapter. Often, your national headquarters wisely will advise you to suspend the accused brother's membership until after the investigation is completed. You are not to pass judgment on your brother or the merits of the accusation. This is for others to decide. It is not the role of the chapter.

Third, you need to keep the brotherhood out of the situation. The entire brotherhood should refrain from public comment until after the investigation. The chapter should fully cooperate with the university and the authorities in the investigation, however.

Finally, realize that if a sexual assault crime does happen at your chapter house, there is a good chance you will lose your charter and be shut down. If your chapter fosters the type of environment in which sexual assault can happen, then it has no place in the university or Greek community. Unless you want to be forever known as the president who got the chapter shut down, then you need to make sure you create a culture in which this type of impropriety is not accepted.

How to Deal with a Suicide

One issue we had to deal with at our university was the suicide of a much-loved but troubled brother of ours. Our president worked with university resources to assure that we knew of the counseling and other services on campus, but he let each person grieve in his own way while continuing to keep the chapter going. Moving forward made it a very strong uniting point.

As an officer in the Air Force, I was deployed to Kuwait. One of my guys had met a girl online *the month* before we deployed, and then he married her. He essentially met the girl, married her, and then told her that he'd see her in six months when we returned home.

About a month into our deployment, the girl when nuts. She decided she wanted to split up. She joined the army. Then she intentionally hurt herself by pushing a cabinet over on her leg in order to be kicked out of boot camp. (She broke the leg).

During this time, the young guy who worked for me became extremely depressed. I had to ask him if he had thoughts of hurting himself. He told me that he used to hurt himself, but he didn't do that kind of thing anymore. However, he was having an especially hard time dealing with this situation. When he said that, I realized that I was way out of my league. I have a big heart and wanted to help, but I am not qualified to deal with someone who is contemplating self-injury. I called in a professional who was able to get the young man the help he needed.

I want to say that this solved all the problems, but it did not. The guy still had to battle depression. It was imperative for me to keep an eye on him, stay engaged in his life, and make sure he followed up and got the help he needed when he needed it.

Here are the three key points from my story that apply to your chapter:

1) Ask the member if he or she is having suicidal thoughts or thoughts of self-injury. In my limited experience, I have found that people who are hurting are desperate to open up to someone. Explain that you care about him or her and are concerned. If the member is having those types of thoughts, he or she will probably tell you.

2) If a member is having suicidal thoughts, get professional help. Even a friend with the best intentions is not properly trained to handle someone with these types of problems. Again, chances are the member is begging for help on the inside. Help him to help himself. Your campus employs professional counselors. If you don't know who those folks are, call your Greek life director. If you are more comfortable

with clergy, call a chaplain on your campus. Then personally make sure the person meets with the counselor. Time is of the essence. Don't waste a second getting the member the help he needs. You don't know how dire the situation is and cannot take the chance of waiting.

3) Follow up. If you got the member the help she needs, you did a good thing. You may have saved a life. But you must continue to be active in this member's life. Continue to be a good friend and check up on her. Help her talk through her problems. Make sure she continues to get the counseling help she needs.

As a leader, your number one responsibility is taking care of those you lead. Stay engaged in your members' lives. Be sure you are sufficiently in tune that you can see if people are having problems. And if problems occur, you need to drop everything in your life to make sure your sister or brother gets the help he or she needs.

The Death of a Member

The most difficult, out-of-the-ordinary situation is the serious illness or death of a member. As unfair as it may be, the chapter is going to look to the president to keep things together. Two chapters in my geographic region (New Jersey) in the last dozen years have had to support members diagnosed with cancer and ultimately deal with the deaths of those members. I've also had chapters in Pennsylvania and New York that have had to deal with members killed in car accidents. Chapter presidents have to be able to maintain themselves and their chapters. It can test even the best leader.

There is no possible way to prepare for a tragedy of this magnitude. You can't really understand the shock and emptiness of this situation unless you have been through it. Obviously, your priorities as a chapter president significantly change if tragedy strikes your brotherhood or sisterhood.

Your first priority is to make sure you are OK. You cannot lead if you are not in a good place. Talk to your trusted advisers and brothers or sisters about the situation. Talk to your parents. Be sure you have a good handle on your emotions because your chapter is going to need your leadership.

Your next priority is to make sure your members have the proper resources to handle the tragedy. Being able to talk about the situation will help many of them get through it. Although some people won't be eager to express their emotions and feelings, as a leader, you must try to facilitate conversations.

You must be especially vigilant for members who are having a more difficult time than most. Everyone reacts to tragedy differently. Some people sink into depression after suffering a loss. Realize that you are not qualified to deal with depression. You are qualified to be a good friend and brother or sister, but depression is a problem that requires professional assistance. Should a member sink into depression, you need to get help for him. Failing to get help for him is not an option.

Fortunately, in my experience with people dealing with depression, it did not take much coercion to get them to talk to a professional. Your school will have a campus resource person who can help. If you don't know who that person is, ask your Greek life adviser. It goes without saying, of course, that there is no need to advertise that a member is having this type of problem.

Your chapter adviser is another valuable resource. A strong adviser probably will not be going through the same emotional upheaval that the undergraduate members are experiencing, and his leadership can help the chapter to heal. As a trusted outsider, the adviser will be able to assess how the chapter is dealing with the situation.

Finally, bring someone in to talk to the chapter about dealing with grief. Again, your school will have someone who can assist. Your members will put up a tough front and say it isn't necessary, and that is OK. Deep down, though, most will appreciate what a grief counselor has to say, and if inviting a counselor to speak helps one person in the chapter, then it will be well worth it.

It is hard to deal with grief, and it is hard to move on. It will do the chapter a lot of good to try to resume normal chapter operations within a reasonable amount of time. The deceased member would want you to have fun and keep doing the things that make your fraternity or sorority great. Continue to do this to honor him or her.

Finally, do something in his or her memory. When a brother died of diabetes, my chapter dedicated our annual golf tournament to his memory and donated the proceeds to organizations that fight that disease. Giving the members something productive to focus on will help with the healing process.

CONCLUSION

Thank you for reading *The Chapter President*. If you liked to book, please consider leaving feedback on Amazon. I recommend you check out my other books too. *The Fraternity Leader: The Complete Guide to Improving your Chapter* has been very popular. It describes how I would run a fraternity if I had the opportunity to do it all over again. *The Fraternity Handbook* is a compilation of the very best articles posted on www.thefraternityadvisor.com and contains a ton of great information that will help you grow as a Greek leader.

Being the president of a Greek chapter is a daunting responsibility. However, it can be incredibly rewarding. I sincerely hope this book gave you some tools that will help you to become a strong leader and a successful president. If there is ever anything I can do to help you, please do not hesitate to send me an e-mail at info@thefraternityadvisor.com.

Fraternally,

Pat

Made in the USA
Middletown, DE
23 April 2019

Seniors' interests and priorities have changed. They are now focusing on graduation and getting a job. They are probably in a steady relationship, and the last thing their significant other wants to do is to chill at the house.

When seniors don't have an influential role in the planning of chapter events, the chapter tends to hold events that cater to the younger members. This further dissuades the older member from coming around. And when older members do come around, they usually catch a ration of grief from younger members who have contributed a tenth of what the older member has in his time in the chapter.

It is pretty easy to see why older members stay away. But if your chapter sounds like what I just described, then shame on you. As the president of your chapter, it is your job to make sure all members feel they are getting value from their membership. That means you need to have events that keep both the younger members and older members happy.

Fortunately, the older members aren't difficult to please. They don't want much, and if they stuck around until senior year, they obviously feel a deep connection to the chapter. Make it a point to toss them a bone every once in a while by having events that they would like. Obvious ideas of events that older members would want to attend are tailgate parties at football games and semiformal and formal date functions. Many older members like stay active in athletics, so be sure there is room for them on the intramural teams.

The biggest thing you can do is to make sure they feel appreciated when they do come to the house. If they feel welcome, and they know that the members are genuinely glad to see them, then chances are they will make it a point to come around more often.